# HERITAGE & HOPE

## The Legacy and Future of the Black Family in America

*by Howard and Wanda Jones*
*with Dave and Neta Jackson*

Since this book has a dual authorship, for clarity's sake the text is from the viewpoint of Howard Jones.

# VICTOR BOOKS®

A DIVISION OF SCRIPTURE PRESS PUBLICATIONS INC.
USA CANADA ENGLAND

Unless otherwise indicated, Scripture references are from the *Holy Bible, New International Version,* © 1973, 1978, 1984, International Bible Soci ety. Used by permission of Zondervan Bible Publishers. Other references are from the *Authorized (King James) Version* (KJV).

Copy Editor: James R. Adair
Cover Designer: Mardelle Ayres

### Library of Congress Cataloging Data

Jones, Howard.
    Heritage & hope: the legacy and future of the Black family in America /
by Howard & Wanda Jones with Dave & Neta Jackson.
        p.        cm.
    Includes bibliographical references (p.        ).
    ISBN 0-89693-771-2
    1.  Afro-American families. I. Jones, Wanda. 1923-
II. Jackson, Dave. III. Jackson, Neta. IV. Title. V. Title: Heritage and
hope.
    E185.86, J652      1992                                              91-40077
    306.8'08996073 — dc20                                               CIP

1   2   3   4   5   6   7   8   9   10   Printing/Year   96   95   94   93   92

# Contents

To Our Grandchildren:

Timothy and Ryan Sanders,
Jonathan, Dean and Andy Thornton,
and April Kelly, who represent
a new generation.

# Foreword

Speaking from a lifetime of experience, and drawing upon their own rich heritage as black Americans, Howard and Wanda Jones in this book have set forth with candor, wisdom, and sympathy the problems besetting the black community. Unlike so many commentators, they are not content to examine the symptoms but they analyze in depth the root causes of those problems. Their analysis is hard-hitting, perceptive—and at times controversial. Nevertheless, by highlighting the crucial importance of the family and pinpointing the pressures which have torn apart so many black families today, the Joneses convincingly demonstrate why there can be no lasting solution to the social and moral crises of our time apart from the renewal of the family unit.

They correctly note, however, that there can be no effective renewal of the family apart from spiritual renewal, and the principles God has given us in His Word. Through a careful study of the biblical principles for family living, they point the way to the solution. Although written mainly for the black community, this book sets forth in a practical and clear way the spiritual foundations which should undergird every family.

For many years, it has been my privilege to have Howard Jones as a member of my Team, and I have always had the deepest respect and admiration for his ministry and his family. I am delighted he and his wife, Wanda, have written such a timely and practical book. This could well become one of the most significant books of the decade—not just for blacks, but for all Americans regardless of ethnic background. It deserves the widest possible circulation.

Billy Graham
Montreat, North Carolina

# Preface

The American family is struggling to keep its head above water in an era of unprecedented stress. For every two couples getting married today there is also one divorce. And 50 percent of American children today will live at least part of their growing-up years in a single-parent household. As more and more mothers enter the work force, there is a growing percentage of children who spend a major portion of each week in day-care facilities or as latch-key children. Alcoholics and drug addicts are packing out treatment centers as people struggle to keep from passing the sins of one generation on to the next.

Nowhere have these problems so devastated the family as in the black community, particularly in the inner city. What concerns us is the slow, yet persistent deterioration of African-American culture and the loss of the high moral and spiritual values that have seen blacks through the dark days of slavery, repression, and racism. The foundation that held the black community together during its bleakest hours was the family, rooted more often than not in a deep family faith, hand in hand with the black church.

Today that foundation is disintegrating from within and without. Even as we have gained (and lost) civil rights, even as more black Americans are achieving the American dream, even as black athletes and music stars rise, we are

7

losing great numbers of our children to poverty, drugs, and hopelessness. We are losing our black men to unemployment, underemployment, drug use and drug dealing, alcoholism, AIDS, violence, homicide, and prison. We are losing our black women to teenage pregnancy, as they drop out of school and begin an endless cycle of welfare or try to live on pauper's wages. We are losing the influence and strength of the black church which once helped bind us together.

As individuals, families, and churches in the black community, we need to return to our spiritual roots. We need to make family a priority. We need to lift up the role models of solid black families who have become the role models for the new generation. We must give back to our children and communities what we have been given. We must have hope.

The church of Jesus Christ and the people of Jesus Christ have the answer for the crisis in the black family. But we have been slow to do our job. Historically, the black church has been a place of refuge, a place where our people could go and have their fears relieved and their pain comforted. But the black church must also become a place of development—a place where we not only find strength in the foundation of our faith, Jesus Christ, but a place where we can learn to make our way as whole, nurturing families.

In this book, we focus on our heritage of strong, black families before grappling with the crisis which is threatening their very existence. We explore what is happening to our black men, and challenge men to fulfill the role only they can fill as husbands and fathers. We examine the foundations for once again building strong black families, and from there consider the roles of husbands and wives, fathers and mothers, the importance of spiritual and moral values, discipline and guidance of children, the role of the black church, and what we blacks must do to take control of our own destiny.

Central to this book is our relationship with Jesus Christ. Without His help and direction and obedience to the Word of God no family is complete. He is the building block on which all other issues rest. He offers hope for all families who are suffering.

Let us begin.

# Acknowledgements

We wish to give a special word of appreciation to our friends at Victor Books who encouraged us to get started on this book—Mark Sweeney, vice president; Carole Sanderson Streeter; and Mavis Sanders.

We sincerely thank David and Neta Jackson, who faithfully worked with us during the long months of research and writing; and special thanks also to Billy Graham for writing the foreword, and his personal secretary, Stephanie Wills for her help. We also appreciate the work of our friend Jim Adair, the Victor Books senior editor who edited the book, and Mardelle Ayres, who designed the cover.

And, finally, we wish to express our gratitude to our children and their spouses and Pastor Charles B. Mayle and the congregation of the Oberlin Alliance Church for their love and prayer support when we needed it.

A.W. Tozer said, "The best book is one that starts us on a train of thought that carries us beyond the book itself." We send forth this book and pray that God will use it for His glory, to inspire, encourage, and help those who read it.

## -1-
## The Heritage of the Black Family

*O let us all from bondage flee.*
*Let my people go,*
*And let us all in Christ be free.*
*Let my people go.*
*T r a d i t i o n a l*

**"I want my children** to drink from Lake Erie," Jane Martin said.

"Lake Erie? What's wrong with living in Virginia?" her husband, Henry, shot back. "We're doing all right now."

"It's been my dream, ever since I heard General Lee say he wouldn't be satisfied till his horse drank from Lake Erie. This is also my ambition and goal for our family."

But to understand the long trek that took my great-grandmother Jane Martin by foot, train, and boat from Virginia to Ohio, where I grew up, we have to back up a few years before the Civil War.

### Discovering Our Roots

In 1828 a slave baby named Jane Robinson was born in Bedford County, Virginia. Like many babies born in slavery, she was given the last name of her master, George Robinson. When Jane was twenty years old, she was given to George Robinson's daughter Polly as her property when Polly married Granville Pullin in 1848.

Jane lived with the Pullins for seventeen years. During this time, Gran Pullin bought a slave named Henry Martin from his neighbor Tom Martin, and Henry and Jane were married. One daughter was born to them during slavery; she was three and a half years old when General Lee surrendered. Just after Lee's surrender, another daughter, named Mary, was born. Mary Martin was my grandmother.

From Grandmother Mary (later Mary Mungeon), my brother Clarence and I heard the stories of how the newly freed Martin family, with their small daughters, hired out to a man named Wink Willard. The family was very poor, and received part of Willard's crop in payment for their labor. Willard also gave the Martins an ox; from this cow my great-grandmother Jane eventually raised five yoke of oxen!

When little Mary was three, the Martins moved on by ox cart and hired themselves out to a man named McHenry Williamson. Henry and Jane worked till harvest, with the understanding that they would receive a share of the crop. But at harvest they were run off and given nothing.

Discouraged, hungry, and their family increasing, the Martins settled on a farm leased by a "colored man," Israel Sanders, who was too ill to work the land. Henry and Jane worked very hard without tools or horses to raise a tobacco crop. At the end of the season, they harvested eight tobacco houses full of first class tobacco! The Martins were tired but proud and happy; two-thirds of this crop belonged to them, one-third to Sanders. Maybe things were going to work out after all.

A few nights after harvest, they were awakened by pounding at their door. It was a white neighbor, Mr. Overstreet. "Henry, I was in town today at the court, and I heard that the magistrate is planning to levy your crop to get Sanders' back rent, which hasn't been paid in three years." Mr. Overstreet saw the dismay register in Henry's and Jane's eyes. "Do you have anyone who can help you get the crop out of here?"

Henry thought. "My father lives back in Bedford County. I could get there by morning if I had a horse."

"Well, then, take mine, man," said Overstreet. "The magistrate will be here in a couple days."

On Overstreet's horse, Henry rode all night. By the next night, Henry's father and some other friends drove eight long wagons into the Sanders' farm and loaded the crop.

The next day as the magistrate rode toward Israel Sanders' farm, he met wagon after wagon of tobacco. Hurrying on to the farm, all the magistrate found was the third of the crop that belonged to Sanders.

The Martin family settled once again in Bedford County, Virginia, and the family grew to eleven children. But Jane never forgot her ambition—to go north. That was always the goal held up before the children: "Someday you'll drink from Lake Erie."

On April 4, 1881, Jane, young Mary (who was about sixteen years old), and Jane's stepfather, George Dickison, set out to go north. Not yet convinced, Henry stayed behind with the other children. It would have been a short trip by train, but black folks weren't generally welcome on the train, so they traveled three days on foot. In Buchanan, Virginia, they again tried to get the train, but here they feared for their very lives. Unknown to them, a Negro had recently committed a crime, and any black face was a threat. A crowd began to gather; chants of "Kill 'em! Hang 'em!" terrified the three travelers.

Had it not been for Grandpa Dickison's crooked legs, there's no telling what may have happened. But suddenly a white man pushed his way through the crowd and said, "George?" Grandpa Dickison's face lighted in recognition. The man was the nephew of the "other" George Dickison, the landowner for whom Grandpa had worked as a boy and for whom he was named. Young George had broken his legs and they had never been set properly, and it was these crooked legs that gave away his identity.

The nephew helped the trio get out of town to a safe place for the night, from where they continued their journey. They arrived at the Ohio River in Huntington, West Virginia with only seventy-five cents between them, hardly enough to pay for passage; but a boat captain let them ride on the lower deck of his river boat free.

When the boat nosed up to the dock in Ironton, Ohio, about fifteen miles west of Huntington, night had fallen and sleet was pelting their faces. They had no friends, no home, but as they climbed the hill toward the town, Jane assured her stepfather, "Jesus is with us and will provide for us." Then she began to sing, "Where He leads me I will follow."

At the top of the hill they inquired about lodging and went to the home of the town blacksmith. When they asked for a place to stay, the blacksmith said, "My wife's sick and we got twenty boarders—railroad men—wanting supper. Can you cook?" Jane pitched right in, and by morning word had gotten around and five different people wanted Jane to work for them.

In a month, she sent home twenty dollars—more than they could have saved in a year in Virginia. Henry was finally convinced and agreed to bring the other children.

After three months in Ironton and sending sixty dollars and a box of clothes to her family back home, Jane followed her stepfather, who had already gone ahead to Cincinnati; this time she and Mary paid for first-class passage. The men working on the narrow gauge railroad needed room and board, so Jane rented a house large enough for thirty-five boarders. When the railroad contractors were done in Cincinnati, Jane moved to Cleveland and opened a boarding house there.

Cleveland! Right on the shores of Lake Erie. Jane Martin's dream had almost come true. The contractors built a boarding house on Paper Mill Hill, and Jane fed as many as 250 railroad men. Soon she was able to send for the rest of her family. Reunited once more, the Martin family triumphantly went to the shores of Lake Erie and had a drink. They had reached their goal!

### And Then the Church

In two years the Martin and Dickison families, along with a third family, the McGees, moved to Oberlin, Ohio, the home of Oberlin College, about thirty-five miles southwest of Cleveland. In the mid-1880s, about four hundred folk in Oberlin, nearly one-fifth of the population, were black. Some attended the white churches, and others the two black Methodist churches that had been organized. The Martins, Dickisons, and McGees, however, were not Methodists by persuasion, so they began holding prayer meetings and Sunday School in their homes. More and more people began attending these cottage prayer meetings and it became apparent that a more formal organization was necessary, giving birth in 1886 to the Mt. Zion Baptist Church.

My great-grandmother Jane Martin died in 1908; my great-grandfather Henry died nine years later. My grandmother Mary, who was about twenty when her family moved to Oberlin, had married my grandfather Goglin Jones in Cleveland before they also came to Oberlin to live. Their son Howard was my father. Grandmother Mary later married Matthew Lewis after my grandfather's death, and still later married Samuel Mungeon after Matthew Lewis died. My grandmother was a wig maker and had a shop on Main Street in Oberlin.

### An Important Heritage

What does it mean to me to piece together this history from stories told by my grandmother Mary, contained in a typewritten document in the Oberlin College Archives, a book of Oberlin history,[1] and a history of the Mt. Zion Baptist Church? It gives me a foundation. My forebearers had a strong family life, even in slavery. With the support of family and helpful neighbors, both black and white, they survived hard times and overcame the barriers that stood in their way. Both mother and father contributed to the family's support and survival. They set goals and did what they had to do to reach them. They were devout Christian believers; their faith in God was strong. Their faith was not simply a private matter, but they felt it important to gather with other believers for fellowship, worship, and teaching; and they believed in the training of children. A church rose in Oberlin, Ohio from their efforts, a lasting heritage to future generations.

Each generation must choose for itself to keep alive its heritage and build on it if it is solid, or to let it go. There is nothing automatic about it, just as there is nothing automatic about our salvation. As a teenager and a saxophonist in a local dance band, I thought the "faith of my fathers" and church membership was good enough for me; my goal was to become famous as a jazz musician. But it was Wanda Young, the girl I loved, who showed me I must choose for myself to let Jesus be my Lord and Savior, to give Him my talents and whole life to God. When I did, I also had to surrender my plans to God—and He had different plans for me, more wonderful than I could ever have imagined. He called me to be a preacher. When I said yes to God, I never dreamed that would mean pastoring two churches and later becoming the first black associate evangelist with the Billy Graham Team, with a worldwide preaching and radio ministry.

I had to choose, but the foundation my parents and grandparents and great-grandparents laid played an important role in that choice. Who I am, what I believe, and what my wife and I did as parents to help lay the foundation for the choices our children and grandchildren will make for their lives and family. My wife, Wanda, also has a heritage of which she is proud, and in her account which follows, note how her parents influenced her life.

## On Her Knees

I was born in 1923 in Oberlin, the youngest of nine children. My parents, James and Florie Young, both enjoyed music and sang in our church choir. They also spent evenings with neighbors and church friends, often gathered around the pot-bellied stove in our living room. As the youngest child, I was usually sent to bed; but more often than not, I lay on the floor of the bedroom I shared with my older sister, Ruth, listening to the talk and stories of the adults through the hot air register.

This is how I learned that my Italian grandfather passed on his love of music and a respect for their individual talents to his nine daughters and, finally, a son, my father. This is how I learned that Grandpa Young was frustrated that there were subtle—and not so subtle—limits put on what his children could do, just because he had married a black woman. This is how I learned that not everyone was as safe and protected as we were in our integrated neighborhood there in Oberlin. I didn't understand the stories some of the adults told about "the South"—drunken mobs and lynching and burning crosses.

My father was a cook, a kind and gentle man, except when injustice triggered a fiery temper. One day my father stomped into the house.

"James," said my startled mother, "what on earth are you doing home?"

I had never seen my father so steamed up. He paced up and down the room. We knew that his boss at the restaurant, Mr. Zion, often rode his employees hard, yelling and calling them names. This time he had gone too far. Then, suddenly, my father sighed and dropped into a chair. "I'd had enough, Florie. So I . . . put him in the cooler."

**17**

"Mr. Zion! In the cooler! Is he still there?"

My father grinned and nodded.

But my mother didn't think it was funny. At her urging, my father went back to the restaurant and opened the door to the cooler. Mr. Zion's first words were, "You're fired!"

"You don't have to fire me," my father said, "because I quit!" He took off his cook's coat and started out the door. The prospect of actually losing one of his best cooks rapidly brought Mr. Zion to his senses. I never knew what happened next, except that my father didn't lose his job and no more was said about it.

My mother, on the other hand, seemed to have infinite patience and never had a hard thing to say about anyone. As the youngest, I often had her to myself after school, and I loved to help her in the kitchen and just talk. When I pushed her with questions about why white kids seemed to have more privileges than black kids, she just said, "Remember, Wanda, that God made you special too. There's always going to be people who don't like you because of the color of your skin, but that's their problem, not yours. God made the whole world and He made people all different colors. It just so happens that there are more white people than black people in America, but in God's eyes they're all the same."

My mother herself treated everyone alike. My white friends were just as welcome at our house as my black friends. When a neighbor was sick, whether white or black, Mama took care of their children and helped prepare food. But gradually I began to realize that the reverse was not always true. One of my white friends took me to her house only when her mother wasn't home. And once when I recovered from a serious bout with measles and pneumonia, I realized that only black friends and neighbors had come to help.

"Why, Mama?" I asked during one of our kitchen talks.

"Wanda, honey," she said, "we can't go through life

wondering why other people don't do what they're supposed to do. We just have to make sure we're doing what Jesus wants *us* to do."[2]

Mama's love for Jesus and her obedience to God were more important to her than petty hurts and slights. I was never encouraged to dwell on self-pity, or to let bumps in the road keep me from the right path. Her father—my grandfather—had been a preacher in a little church in South Carolina when Mama was my age. "I still remember the day I understood what my daddy was saying about our need for Jesus," she told me one day. "It changed my life to realize I had a Savior who died for *my* sins and who understood all the struggles and problems of growing up. I've been talking to Jesus ever since."

But when I was twelve years old, my mother died of spinal meningitis. I was devastated. For years I was angry at God for taking her away from me. Her death seemed to take the old spitfire out of my father as well. When my father and I were on a bus trip to Chicago to visit his sister, two belligerent white passengers who got on in Indiana demanded that we move to the back of the bus so they could have our seats. I knew my father was angry, and I begged him just to move and not make a scene. We sat in the back of the bus in stony silence for the rest of the trip.

In Chicago he talked out his anger with his sister and her husband, but instead of pacing and blowing, he just seemed tired and spent. Two years later he moved back to South Carolina, leaving me in the care of my oldest brother Alden and my sister Ruth.

I didn't date much in high school—not until I met Howard Jones, that is. Though I had seen him around school, I didn't sit up and take notice until I heard him play his saxophone in a church service. He and his brother, Clarence, a fine trumpeter, kept busy on weekends with a local dance orchestra. By our senior year our future dreams began to include each other. Howard wanted to pursue a career as a musician. All I knew is that I loved his wonderful music with the band.

My brother Alden made me attend church regularly, but I had lost personal interest since Mama died. Then a few weeks into my senior year, the pastor of our church, Elsie Gatherer, personally invited all the teenagers to attend a series of special meetings—a revival. "The music is going to be great," she gently encouraged. I went with my cousin and a couple friends and sat in the back.

The music, provided by students from Biola Institute in California, more than met my expectations. But even more than the music, I saw something else—these musicians were doing what they were doing, not for themselves, but for Jesus. As each one shared a testimony, I realized that some of them also had hurts like mine. But instead of being bitter, they found strength and comfort in God's love. Not only that, but they seemed to have found joy in giving God their talents, their lives, their futures.

I kept going back, and at the end of the week I made a decision: what Jesus Christ wanted for my life was what I wanted too. And suddenly the empty places in my life seemed to fill up. This was what Mama had tried to tell me. I knew she was rejoicing in heaven over my decision, and I knew that someday we would meet in heaven again.

When I tried to share my newfound joy with Howard, however, he was accepting but didn't seem to understand the turn my life had taken. I realized that our plans didn't seem right to me anymore. He came to church with me, we talked . . . but we were growing apart. Finally I told him, "Howard, I love you, but I love Jesus more. Whatever I do with my life, I want to do for Jesus."

It was painful for both of us, but I had to let Howard go and give him—our relationship—over to God. But I prayed hard and asked others to pray too. God is so faithful. Before the year was out Howard had asked Jesus to be Lord of his life as well as his Savior!

For a while, he continued on with the orchestra, even though God had impressed him to quit. One night, however, his fellow musicians pressured him to attend a night club on Lake Erie, where a famous orchestra appeared. I advised Howard not to go, but he felt otherwise. Later Howard and his friends entered the ballroom, but the music and the dancers did not satisfy him. Suddenly he felt as if he were suffocating with deep conviction from the Holy Spirit. He finally stumbled outside for a breath of fresh air. On that clear and beautiful moonlit night, he knew that God was dealing with him. "OK, Lord," he said, "I'll quit the band and accept Your call to preach the Gospel."

When Howard rushed to my house to tell me, I knew then that God was knitting us together for His purpose—whatever that might be. Together we went to Nyack Bible College and then in 1944 we married. Howard was first called to pastor Bethany Christian and Missionary Alliance Church in Harlem, New York; that inner-city ministry grew to include Saturday night rallies, a radio broadcast, and a summer camp. Six years and three daughters later we accepted a call to pastor a church in Cleveland, Ohio, where a son and another daughter were born. Howard's radio broadcasts, which were rebroadcast on radio station ELWA in Monrovia, Liberia, eventually led to a three-month evangelistic tour in West Africa, which in turn in 1957 led Dr. Billy Graham to ask Howard to join his team as an associate evangelist. God was indeed using Howard to take His Word around the world!

Our children—Cheryl, Gail, Phyllis, David, and Lisa—are familiar with the story of my telling their father, "Howard, I love you, but I love Jesus more." By the world's standards it was a risk; by God's standards, obedience to His Word always results in the very best. All of our children have opened their hearts and lives to the Lord; God in turn has provided each one with a Christian spouse whose desire is also to serve the Lord. As I see them establishing Christian homes and building on the foundation we tried to provide for them, I praise God for the heritage of a Christian family.

My heart aches for the many children growing up in fatherless homes today. Countless mothers struggle to be parent and provider alone. Standing on street corners all over urban America are fathers who feel life is a dead-end street, whose lives are at risk through crime, drugs, poor health. I am especially sad for the young people who have never learned how to set goals and plan for the future, but who take the quick way to money and pleasure through drugs and sex—a shortcut that leads nowhere.

Still I have hope. Let us remember that our God is the God of the impossible. He is able to redeem even the most hopeless situations. But we must allow Him to become Lord of our lives and our families. We must return to the Bible as our guidebook and be obedient to His commands. To our children we must pass on a Christian faith, our proud heritage, and solid moral and educational values to give them a foundation on which to build. In the love of Christ we must reach out to those who are hurting—one to one, family to family, healing church to hurting community.

**Something to think about:**
1. What are some of the values you pass on that your mother or father or grandparents told you were important in life?
2. How have you encouraged your parents, grandparents, aunts and uncles to share stories about their lives and the lives of *their* relations when gathered together with your children?
3. What were the reasons for the family moves that have happened in your family over the last two generations? How have they affected the general welfare of your family?
4. Do you teach your children black history?

**- 2 -**

**Strengths
of the
Black
Family**

*Looking back through the years,
There were joys and some tears.
There were losses and gains;
There was laughter and some pains.
All is well, all is well.*
  J a m e s   H e n d r i x

**That the black family is struggling** today is, in one sense, nothing new. The black family in America has been under attack for 300 years. First, families were violently uprooted against their will from their African homeland, and carried in chains to a life of servitude in a strange land. In many cases, husbands were separated from wives, mothers from children, on the auction block. The conditions of slavery made it difficult for black men to care for and protect their families. Even after emancipation, racial discrimination, repression, and poverty inhibited many blacks from being able to adequately support their families. In some instances, Northern cities did not prove to be the promised land, but rather became enclaves (ghettos) of a dispirited people, trapped in a vicious cycle of unemployment, welfare dependency, broken homes, illegitimacy, crime, and delinquency. Black Americans have had to fight every inch of the way for their civil rights.

Many would characterize black families today, especially those of the black underclass, as disintegrating, socially disorganized, unstable, and deficient in being able to carry out essential family functions—in short, an interpretation that focuses on the weaknesses of the black family situation. However, that black families have survived *at all* given the overwhelming odds against them is a testimony and a witness—not to their weakness, but to the inherent strengths of the black family in America.

### Basic Family Strengths

Albert J. McQueen, who teaches sociology at Oberlin College, has written in a paper titled "Adaptations of the Urban Black Family" that "family casualties and failures have occurred and will continue to occur, but . . .they should not be allowed to detract from accomplishments of heroic proportions under . . . trying circumstances."[1]

McQueen goes on to quote Robert B. Hill, who lists five basic strengths of black families in his little book, *Strengths of Black Families*:[2]

1. *Strong kinship bonds.* Extended family sentiments and ties tend to be maintained, particularly among poor people. They are manifested in a willingness to aid relatives in need and to accept both kin and nonkin children and adult relatives into the family.

2. *Strong work orientation.* This is revealed in attitudinal studies and the high proportion of working wives in husband-wife families.

3. *Adaptability of family roles.* This primarily involves egalitarian decision-making in family affairs, which has been found to be more characteristic of black families than the popular image of matriarchy or wife-dominance.

4. *High achievement orientation.* The desire to achieve in education, occupation, and income tends to be pronounced among parents and their children, though it often is not matched by an equally strong sense of efficacy or optimistic expectations of success.

5. *Positive orientation toward religion.* While not all blacks are religious any more than any other segment of the population, the church is a central institution in the black community, a bulwark for the maintenance of family values of respectability, perseverance, and achievement.

In the midst of a crisis that concerns us deeply, it is important—nay, essential—to remember that crisis in the black family is not all there is, *and* it was not always so. Not only do solid black families who are successfully raising their children and passing on faith, values, and traditions exist in all social strata today, but it is the black family itself that has been our strength through decades of adversity from every side.

In any crisis we must first regain our footing to see what our foundation is. If our goal is to restore the black family, we have to know what it is we want to preserve. To go forward into the future, we have to wisely look back at the past to know what our heritage is.

Wise King Solomon wrote, "Where there is no vision, the people perish" (Prov. 29:18, KJV). We believe it is important to reclaim the vision of family held by our parents and grandparents, so that we can pass that vision on to our children and grandchildren.

### Traditional Black Family Structure

In the hundred-year period after the end of slavery, the majority of black families experienced basic stability, with married couples raising their children until the children established their own families.

The African heritage of the American black family also placed a high value on blood ties, including other family members in the family system. Thus, while the *nuclear* family has been at the core of the black family, the *extended* family is also an important strength, often including one or both grandparents and one or more unmarried aunts and uncles or cousins living in the family unit. If a parent is lost to death or divorce, the children are enfolded into the extended family and raised, often by a grandparent, but also by aunts and uncles.

This commitment to family has another advantage that is seldom acknowledged. The illegitimacy rate among African Americans is truly at tragic proportions—over half of all births—but what is not noticed is that relatively fewer of these babies are being aborted than among the white population. Even when they are born to teenage moms, more are being raised by grandparents and aunts and uncles and—to the best of their ability—the teenage moms. According to Andrew Edwards of Cleveland State University, "Of the 1.6 million abortions performed annually in the United States, most are obtained by young, white, unmarried women—63 percent are age twenty-four or younger; 70 percent are white, and 81 percent are unmarried. . . . It should be noted that the majority of the black community's pregnancies are within the lower socio-economic strata—the group that has the lowest abortion rate. . . . Comprehensive data suggests that blacks definitely do have more babies proportionately out of wedlock. But whites have a larger number and a proportionately greater acceptance, of abortion as a means of birth control."[3]

Another form of the traditional family might be called the *augmented* family—children incorporated into the family system without benefit of blood ties or formal adoption. There is among minority peoples a strong sense of responsibility and caring for one another even beyond ties of blood and marriage.

Andrew Billingsley, professor of African-American studies at the University of Maryland, in his book *Climbing Jacob's Ladder,*[4] recounts a story told by the Rev. Otis Moss, senior pastor of the Olivet Institutional Baptist Church, Cleveland, whose mother died when he was quite young. His father, who did his best to care for his motherless children, died tragically in an automobile accident a few years later. While young Otis stared in shock at the car wreckage, a neighbor woman came by, took him by the arm, and said, "Come home with me." There was never anything formal or legal, but Otis grew up in this family, went to college, and was launched into his adult life, all with the benefit of a caring family.

These are variations which have helped make up the strong traditional black family structure, with both fathers and mothers (as well as other family members) providing care, passing on faith and values, and being role models.

## The Importance of Role Models

Some time ago we clipped a fine article entitled "A Thank You for Gifts Only Parents Can Give," written by William Raspberry, the widely read black syndicated columnist. The article gives a glimpse of the parents who served as role models for a wise and articulate journalist:[5]

Dear Mom and Dad,
Thanks for the gifts. No, not for the things you've bought over the years, though I'm grateful for that too. What I have in mind are those long-ago gifts that have made so much difference in my life.

I'm thinking, for instance, of Mom's gift of the love of language. If my writing displays any grace or rhythm, I owe it to the fact that Mom (English teacher and amateur poet) sparked my interest in the way words work, taught me to hear both the sound and sense of words and to use the one to reinforce the other.

You've probably forgotten those pre-television evenings when we used to sit around the fire and listen as she read poetry, her own and others': Frost and Browning, Lowell and Langston Huges and James Weldon Johnson, Whittier and Sandburg, Dunbar's dialect and even Eugene Fields and that stuff out of "Poems Teachers Ask For."

If Mom's poetry-readings taught me style, it was Dad (the shop-teacher pragmatist) who taught me substance. Both end tables and arguments, he taught, were shakey and worthless unless they stood squarely on all four legs. Both had to be planned and thought about and tested if they were to be worthwhile. . . .

But it isn't just my writing that has been shaped by your gifts. My view of the world is forever influenced by Mom's passion and Dad's cool examination. Neither of you ever resorted to name-calling, knowing that it was better and more satisfying to alter an enemy's view, however subtly, than to engage in ad hominem argument. And you gave me the grace to acknowledge that even our enemies are right some of the time.

Thanks, too, for the courage you gave me. You must have found it painful to raise your black children in the terribly limited environment of segregated Mississippi: the second-rate schools, the second-class citizenship, the total disfranchisement (I was in college before you voted in your first election). And yet neither of you ever dwelt on racism. I suppose you took it for granted that we were aware of the racism that permeated Mississippi society and took it as your duty to give us the strength and self-confidence to prosper in that atmosphere, to make the most of our too-limited opportunities.

As a result, my brother, my sister, and I never thought of ourselves as hopeless victims but as masters of our own fate.

Thanks for that.

And thanks for your emphasis on service, and on your moral and ethical standards, an emphasis that you taught by both precept and example. The "values clarification" nonsense they teach nowadays would have struck you as silly. To be sure, there were moral and ethical dilemmas to be dealt with, and you taught me how to work through them. But you also taught me that I didn't have to work through every single decision. Some things were simply right or wrong. . . .

I know it must embarrass you for me to say these things so publicly. But I think a columnist's readers have the right to know who he is, and how he came to be who he is.

Thanks for everything.

Role models. How many times have we heard, "It's not what you say that influences your children; it's who you are and what you do"? We need to apply this adage from two perspectives.

*First, for ourselves,* to honor those in our families and communities who have modeled faith in God, integrity, morality, self-esteem, hard work, and perseverance. Since we don't come from perfect families, we may need to search for these role models who belong to us; but they are there.

*Second, for our children,* to commit ourselves to being the kind of people we want our children to be. Of course we want our children to reach higher and go further than we have gone; but we cannot expect our children to make up for our character weaknesses if we harbor bitterness or anger, sit all day in front of the TV, are hypocritical, squander time and money on drinking and partying, and never read the Bible or pray together as a family. We live our lives, not just for ourselves, but even more for our children and others who look up to us.

**Some things to think about and do:**
1. How far back can you trace your family tree? Do your children know about these ancestors, who they are and what they did?
2. Plan a family reunion sometime in the near future. Listen to the older folks. Get them to tell stories. If possible, tape-record these conversations.
3. If your parents are still living, write them a letter expressing thanks for some of the "gifts" they gave you. You might use the letter by William Raspberry as a sample.

## -3-
## Pressures
## on the
## Black
## Family

*This world is one great battlefield,*
*With forces all arrayed;*
*If in my heart I do not yield,*
*I'll overcome someday.*
C. A l b e r t  T i n d l e y

**There is an old African proverb,** "If you knock the nose, the eye cries." No doubt this has been applied in myriad of ways, but one thing it surely means: if some in the black community suffer, all suffer. The black family is in crisis— possibly the biggest crisis it has faced since mothers, fathers, and children were ripped from their African homelands 300 years ago—and all of us are affected.

Ever since the publication in 1965 of the controversial Moynihan report on the black family, there have been ominous warnings that the very survival of the black family is at stake. Many of these studies and reports fail to acknowledge the past history of the traditionally strong black family, strengths that have helped black Americans survive through centuries of oppression and hard times. But we are not doing ourselves a favor if we turn a blind eye to the reality of what is happening to the family in our midst. For "when the nose is knocked, the eye cries."

Just as it is important to know our history and the role of the traditionally strong black family in helping black Americans survive and persevere in the midst of external pressures, it is important that we understand the serious nature of the crisis that is upon us. For it is only in understanding the cords that bound us together in the past, and why they are unraveling now, that we will be able to do what we must do for the sake of our children and our future.

### Chicken or the Egg?

The issues affecting the family are complex and interrelated, but they are often addressed as single issues. "The War on Drugs" or "Pro-Choice vs. Pro-Life" dominate the headlines and political rhetoric. The abortion issue especially is fiercely fought on both sides.

Andrew Edwards of Cleveland State University writes: "The use of illicit drugs, teenage rebellious activity, domestic violence, irresponsible sexual behavior, individual depression, chronic anxiety, and certain other emotional disturbances are often termed *social pathology* (or sickness or deviance). However, it is erroneous to view the above as 'social problems.' All of the above are *symptoms* of a problem. The problem is FAMILY DYSFUNCTION."[1]

Other experts see it as the other way around. Poverty and unemployment, decades of oppression and the resulting lack of self-esteem, the abuse of illegal drugs—all of which impact each other—create a combustible mixture which is seriously damaging the black family.

Whichever came first, the chicken or the egg, isn't as important as realizing that these are not isolated problems, nor do they affect isolated people. These problems add up to disaster for the black family; the family system is crumbling, and this impacts the whole black community.

## Economics and Unemployment

That economics plays a definitive role in the stability of the family can be seen in the following 1983 statistics:[2]

- The underclass (nonworking poor) had 75 percent single-parent families, and only 25 percent husband-wife families.
- The working poor had only one-third husband-wife families.
- The working class is still the largest stratum of black families (though the underclass is rapidly catching up). Here fully 60 percent were husband-wife families.
- In the middle class, who tend to be educated, with family incomes between $25,000–$50,000 (1983 dollars), 83 percent were husband-wife families!
- Among the black upper-class, an overwhelming 96 percent were husband-wife families.

Another way to say this would be that even though only 29 percent of poor black families have both a father and mother in the home, a healthy 79 percent of nonpoor black families *are* married couples! It can be argued whether poverty is *a cause or a consequence* of family dissolution, but "a significant decline in the earning power of young black men has contributed significantly to the retreat from marriage and the rise of illegitimacy during the last fifteen years."[3]

Unfortunately, in spite of emancipation, in spite of the civil rights movement, in spite of civil rights legislation, since 1960 unemployment rates for blacks have been consistently double those for whites—and rising. For instance, in 1985 the jobless rate for blacks was 15.1 percent while it was only 6.2 percent for whites.[4]

We cannot overlook that racism and discrimination play a significant role in the economic picture of black families.

There is a great need for job-training programs and educational reforms in city schools, but national priorities and expenditures have been elsewhere. Also, in the last fifteen years or so we've changed from a "hard-producing" country to a "soft-producing" country. In other words, so many of the jobs in steel and other industries, where traditionally there were good tradespeople working, have been lost to automation or as a result of companies moving away. Now it's hard for anybody who doesn't have an education or high skill training to get a good job.

Black males especially have a hard time getting jobs, and unless there's proper employment it's going to hurt the family. All these factors have contributed to the 2.1 million black families (30 percent) who were below the poverty line in 1986.[5]

When there's not enough money coming in to pay the rent or the mortgage, clothe all the kids, and educate them, a lot of other things suffer too. Many of our black families cannot afford good health care. Compared to white children, black children are *twice* as likely to be born prematurely, die during the first year of life, suffer low birth weight, have mothers who received late or no prenatal care, and mothers who die during childbirth.[6]

The lack of adequate health care is one of the reasons why so many black men, women, and children die much earlier than their white counterparts, and it is a factor in the general progress of the black family. If children lack proper medical attention, don't have the proper food, or are without suitable clothes to go to school—and so many of them don't—then how are they going to do well in school? About half of all black children are at least one full grade behind the average white student of the same age. An estimated one third of black students drop out of school before finishing high school. Without a high school diploma, young blacks find that employment prospects plunge, and the cycle spirals downward. It's a very serious problem.

On the other end of the scale, there are a lot of black kids who are bright, with gifts and talents, but their families cannot afford to send them to college. The proportion of black high school graduates who go to college declined from 33.5 percent in 1976 to 26.1 percent in 1987.[7] In our own hometown, Oberlin College, one of the first colleges in the nation to admit blacks, has financial aid programs for African Americans and other minority students, as does many other colleges and universities in the country.

House majority whip William Gray, D-Pa., quit his job in Congress so he could have more influence as head of the United Negro College Fund, which raises money for forty-one historically black colleges. He is also minister of Philadelphia's Bright Hope Baptist Church. Speaking to the press, he said that there was "no greater contribution that I think I can make to my community" than to "widen the doors of education for our . . . black students."

### Welfare

Government has a responsibility when it comes to the economic well-being of its citizens, and especially those at the bottom of the ladder. But good intentions are not always the most helpful.

For instance, we need to take a closer look at the whole welfare system. In some cases it has been a help, and some form of welfare should continue for those who are destitute and need a helping hand. Some black leaders, however, think the welfare program has done more harm than good. Being on the dole too long destroys motivation to achieve or move ahead. Some men take advantage of women on welfare and skip out on their responsibilities to support their children.

Many women receiving ADC (Aid to Dependent Children) have a low self-esteem. They would rather have a good job and make a decent living. Years ago going on welfare was a secret thing, not something to be proud of.

There are blacks today—both men and women—who are working to get off welfare and improve their status. Yet if they have a job, that gets deducted from their welfare, so the motivation is lacking. It becomes a vicious circle, the way it's structured now.

People should be helped to get off welfare. Better to have a system where people are helped with education, childcare, and job training to help them toward jobs. (A new bumper sticker reads, "Childcare Not Welfare.") Both mothers and fathers would feel better about themselves if they had a good job; families would be strengthened; all of society would benefit. Dr. Billingsley, cited earlier, says that the most critical need in the black community "is jobs, jobs, jobs!"

### The Curse of Alcohol and Drugs

We were talking to a young black American mother recently who had just hosted a large family reunion. When we asked how it went, she responded, "We had a good time, a lot of family attended, and there was lots of good food. But I think I may have made an enemy." It turned out that when some of the guests asked where the drinks were, she said that she wasn't serving any alcohol. One of her guests said, "Well, if there's nothing to drink here, I'm leaving." This Christian mother was taking a stand, but it cost her.

The availability of alcohol and drugs in the African-American community is a serious threat to the well-being of our families. Liquor stores are the most common form of small business, and the liquor industry has found a new and potent product for initiating youthful drinkers: wine coolers. Wine cooler sales increased from 150,000 cases in 1982 to 40,000,000 cases in a recent year. And although African Americans represent only 11 percent of the population, our people purchase 30 percent of the Scotch sold in this country. It is estimated that blacks spend $11-12 billion annually on alcohol.[8]

The problems of alcohol—addiction, abuse, loss of employment, disintegration of the family system—has long been documented. But recent decades have put new words in our vocabulary and new demons in our communities: weed (marijuana), acid (LSD), heroin, cocaine, crack, "ice" (powdered speed). In their 1986 special issue on "The Crisis in the Black Family," *Ebony* magazine editors stated, "Clearly no vice does more damage to black people's ability and willingness to fight for better conditions in a racist society than the use of drugs, which systematically sap young blacks' physical and mental strengths."[9]

To many social analysts and black leaders, the problem of drug abuse represents the number-one problem confronting the black community. Not only is an entire generation at risk because of the "drug cancer," through addiction and health-related issues such as AIDS, "but illegal drug use is either directly or indirectly related to much of the crime that plagues the black community."[10] A high percentage of robbery and assault is perpetuated by addicts who need cash to support their habit.

In many of the gangs which infect our inner cities, such as the Crips in Los Angeles and the Stones in Chicago, the terms "gang member" and "drug dealer" are almost synonymous.[11] Competition for the drug market has increased deadly violence between rival gangs, with many innocent young people and men and women caught in the crossfire.

Most insidious, drug trafficking has moved into our schools. While gang members in general are not always easy to identify (unless they deliberately wear gang colors or distinguishing items of clothing), say teachers, those who deal drugs often are. "They wear gold, drive expensive cars (or bicycles, depending on their age), sometimes keep their drugs in school in gym bags, and carry electronic pagers, which let them know when a customer wants to buy drugs. . . . 'For the young kids growing up in poverty, seeing the older kids with sudden wealth becomes a stimulus for them to become involved in drugs,' " said Lorain, Ohio, Detective Tom Cantu.[12]

Eleanor Holmes Norton, formerly the chairperson of the Equal Employment Opportunity Commission in the Carter administration and now the District of Columbia delegate to Congress, agrees. "Kids are very vulnerable to the drug culture, which is the only culture they see around them — at least in the hard-core ghettos." But "there is a special danger for those children that has never existed before: We are passing drugs through our gene pool," Norton adds.

"Now that we see drugs like crack, and women exchanging sex for crack, we are seeing an epidemic of crack babies, cocaine babies, boarder babies. That is the destruction of our community. Many children are being born into the world who will never have a chance for a decent life and will pass that [disadvantage] on to others — that is new, and it is intolerable."[13]

Everyone has his own opinion on the source of the problem. A Washington, D.C. assistant police chief said, "[Youths] want the material things we say people need to be somebody, and they become somebody in the drug trade."[14]

A 29-year-old Los Angeles cab driver who sees a lot of the underside of life, commented: "When a youth decides to sell drugs, that means they've given up on life. It means they don't care past today. They aren't concerned about what their parents or anyone else might think."[15]

Ben Gray, an Omaha TV producer who set up a job-training program for gang members, believes drugs are just a symptom. He blames institutional racism and double standards. "These kids feel locked out of the system," said Gray, whose solution is to "give them a taste of being inside." But the lure of drug money is almost impossible to counter. "What alternative have I got for them?" he says. "What job have I got for a high school dropout that will allow him to get up at noon and make $300 in the afternoon?"[16]

According to a writer in an Akron, Ohio newspaper article, local experts in juvenile delinquency blame the following for the increase in violent offenses, drug trafficking, and gang activity:

- Parents who sell drugs, use drugs or drink to excess.
- The absence of parenting. Many parents don't know where their children are; many children don't know where their parents are.
- Homes in which neither parent shows love for each other or the children.
- Domestic violence and divorce.
- Lack of supervision. Children who are left alone too much and parents who are seldom home. When they are home, they don't set limits. Children never learn to be accountable for their actions.
- Sexual, emotional and physical abuse and neglect of children.[17]

### An Educational Disaster

Obviously, the value system has broken down, not only in our homes and churches, but in our schools as well. And these institutions are all interrelated. What is happening in our homes and churches affects the schools; what's happening in the schools affects the family.

When we were growing up, our dad knew when it was time for report cards! He'd look at the date on the calendar and say, "Howard and Clarence, it's report card time," and there was no avoiding giving an account. Our parents wanted us to excel as students and someday go to college. They cared enough to keep on top of monitoring our progress in consultation with our teachers. Wanda had the same experience. Our parents insisted that we learn how to read and speak properly, and also shared with us interesting events in history. We heard this not only at home, but also from the adults at church.

## Dr. Carson's Story

In his challenging book, *Gifted Hands,* Dr. Ben Carson, the renowned black neurosurgeon, tells the story of how a ghetto kid from Detroit, Michigan, with an uncontrollable temper and a total failure in school, was able to find success in life.[18]

Dr. Carson lauds his Christian mother, who, with a third-grade education, prayed to God for wisdom to help her encourage and motivate her sons to excel in education and achieve outstanding goals in life.

In the home, she limited her sons to only three TV programs a week. She required that they visit the library and read three good books each week on various subjects and report back to her. God eventually rewarded the prayers, patience, and loving concern of this dedicated mother. Ben Carson later graduated with honors from Yale and the University of Michigan Medical School. In 1987 Dr. Carson became a world famous neurosurgeon for the part he played in the miraculous operation on the separation of Siamese twins.

Today, not yet forty, he is the Director of Pediatric Neurosurgery at Johns Hopkins Hospital in Baltimore, Maryland. He's an extremely busy man, but this Christian doctor, a role model, and family man challenges young people across the country to become Christians, get a good education, and honor God in using their gifts and talents for worthwhile pursuits in life. Dr. Carson's mother is also a good example for other parents to follow in rearing their children.

But there are a lot of parents today who don't seem to care what their kids do academically. Sometimes this is because they have not had an education and therefore don't know its value. Sometimes this is because they have been discouraged because the local school system is so poor that it seems impossible to get a good education. And some parents may have concluded that education is not a good bargain—it's too much trouble for the few opportunities that await at the other end.

Unfortunately, peer influence also plays a role. Black students who achieve academically are sometimes accused by their peers of "acting white." It's seen as cool to skip class, to shrug off academic success. But as someone has said, "If you think education is expensive, then try ignorance!"

The lack of motivation in many homes is truly sad. One finds that far too many black young people do not have any aspirations to become outstanding in various fields of professional careers. They perceive that their mothers and fathers are not role models or achievers so why should they want to be something.

Val Jordan, who works with the Navigators' Chicago Urban Ministry, has noticed the same thing. At Wendell Phillips High School there are a high percentage of the students who have never met and talked to an attorney, a doctor (except for medical visits), or a business executive. To them a business man or woman is maybe their landlord or the person who owns the local store. TV images are their only exposure to such professions, and they seem impossibly out of reach.

This lack of inspiration has taken its toll. In 1986 only four blacks in the United States earned Ph.D.s in mathematics, and in all fields of science and engineering, fewer than thirty Ph.D.s were awarded that year to African Americans.[19] Dr. Walter Massey, president of the American Association for the Advancement of Science, says, "There are few black scientists with Ph.D.s because there are few black scientists with bachelor's degrees, because there are few blacks who finish high school who are interested in science."[20]

A few years ago, the National Commission on Excellence in Education released a scathing report which stated that 13 percent of all 17-year-olds and 40 percent of all minority youth were functionally illiterate.[21] In the 10 largest urban cities, the high school dropout rate for black males is 72 percent.[22] Education, which has always been seen as the key to success for a minority people struggling against racism and discrimination, is in danger of rusting in the lock.

There have been and continue to be obstacles of discrimination and lack of opportunity, but what our kids need is inspiration, someone to help them see that becoming *somebody* is possible via an understandable and achievable series of steps from where they are to their desired career goal. And in most cases those steps are education.

The availability of quality schools is essential for good education. Parental involvement in school government, adequate instructional resources, and excellent teachers are all essential for quality education. But one of the commonly overlooked ingredients is the curriculum. It has been well demonstrated that children learn fastest when information is presented in culturally familiar contexts and styles. However, in recent years this has created a dispute. For instance, should they be taught in familiar dialect, or should standard English be used? And because much curriculum often has a bias toward European culture, some people don't want their children taking world history courses or English literature. They want them to take African history courses and study literature by notable African Americans.

In Milwaukee, Wisconsin, the school board has set up two African-American "immersion" schools that are specifically designed for black males—one for the elementary level and the other at the middle-school level. To avoid the Supreme Court's 1954 "separate-but-equal" prohibition, the schools will be open to whites. But in content they will

(1) emphasize black heroes and their contributions, (2) use teaching methods that allow for the different learning styles of black males, and (3) take into account the many home situations without fathers present and provide male "mentoring."[23]

Compensating for the deplorable educational conditions is a good idea, but it is possible to go to extremes. If curriculum needs are changing, it needs a balance for both black and white students. We don't want to produce children who are well-informed in black culture but still unable to compete in broader society. Shelby Steele, a black university professor, says, "When you group people by their race . . . there is a secondary message: that one ought not to identify with the very mainstream that ultimately you want them to succeed in. What you need is the opposite approach—to, as soon as possible, try to mitigate their isolation and have them identify with their American-ness."[24]

A few of the kids who come to the Good Samaritan Center in Cleveland, Ohio and the Christian Outreach Summer Camps, a ministry to all races, can quote the lyrics of the popular rap songs, good and bad . . . but don't know how to read or speak good English. We find that they are growing up without wanting to learn. All they care about is having a good time—no discipline and industry; just take it easy. It's amazing, however, the transformation that takes place in them when they encounter Jesus Christ, the Savior, who gives them motivation, hope, and a new lease on life. Today, unless young people receive a quality education, balanced with moral and spiritual values, we're in danger of losing the next generation to apathy, hopelessness, and despair.

## Breakdown of Community Support

Along with the pressures on the family from external sources has been the breakdown of community support.

When we were growing up, children had many good role models. The people in the community took an interest in all the children on the block. If someone else's daddy or grandmother saw you doing something that wasn't right, they had the permission of your parents to intervene and say, "Don't you do that, or I'm going to tell your parents!" We were afraid to step out of line, because sooner or later Dad or Mom would hear about it, and we'd get in trouble.

I remember the times when our dad used to take my brother, Clarence, and me down to the railroad tracks to see the trains go by. We were utterly fascinated. But he also repeatedly gave us a stern warning. Looking us in the eye he said, "I never want you boys to play down on those tracks, because my brother—your Uncle Harry—was killed by a train years ago." We solemnly promised.

One day when we finished playing a game of marbles, some of us boys just happened to wander down by the railroad tracks. I had two pockets filled with marbles and I was feeling good. Standing there was a pumping car which had been left on a dead track. Oh, boy, we had always envied those railroad men who flew down the tracks on those pumping cars. It was off on a side track that wasn't used, so we had the time of our lives pumping that handle up and down to make the car go.

Unknown to us, someone saw us down on those tracks and went to my father and said, "Just thought you'd like to know your sons are down on the tracks playing with the pumping car." In the midst of our play, we heard a familiar shrill whistle from the top of the embankment. We knew it was Dad. We brought that thing to a screeching halt and jumped off. "Clarence, Howard . . . come up here," he said.

We flew up that hill. "Didn't I tell you not to play on the tracks?" he said.

"But, Dad," we protested, "it's a dead track."

"I know," he said. "But you disobeyed me." He had a belt in his hands, and he had us hopping all the way home, right into the house, as he lashed out at us. And when he got through, I didn't have a single marble left in my pockets.

We got the message. We were taught to obey, and the community backed up our parents. Unfortunately, we've lost that community spirit today. Instead, we pride ourselves on our individualistic society. We don't feel responsible for one another; what someone else's kids do "is none of our business." Parents lack the support of the broader community, and children have generally lost respect for the authority of other adults.

But of course this kind of community influence on our children demands family influence, and the black family, per se, has been struggling internally as we will see in the next chapter.

**Some things to think about and do:**
1. List the three pressures you feel affect your family most and explain what they threaten to do to your family.
2. List the three pressures that affected your family of origin when you were a child. How have these issues changed or remained the same? Explain why you think either has happened.
3. For each pressure your family currently faces, what would be the most practical and likely way of finding release from that pressure?

## - 4 -
## The Crisis in the Black Family

*Nobody knows the trouble I see, Lord,*
*Nobody knows like Jesus.*
        *Traditional*

**Picture a family** in one of America's inner cities. The father has been unemployed for five years. An unskilled worker, his job at the post office was automated; he has since been unable to find work. Two more babies have been added to the family, making three. In his state of residence, two-parent families are not able to receive ADC (Aid to Dependent Children) unless the primary wage-earner is disabled. A single parent, on the other hand, is able to get welfare. Discouraged and angry that he can't support his family, he walks away. Hating himself, this father hits the bottle to ease some of the pain. But the pain doesn't go away, so he moves on. Maybe in some other town, some other place, he can start over.

In the meantime, his sons are growing up without a father. They have no one to teach them the responsibilities of becoming a man, or what it means to be a husband and father. School is hard. What does it have to do with real life anyway? Most of the older kids they know drop out of high school. These young men hang out on the street; no one has a job. Some do have money, however; it comes from selling drugs. The boys look up to the guys selling drugs; they have cars, clothes, parties. Soon the boys are acting as lookouts or passing drugs for older guys in exchange for dollars. Mom looks the other way. She hates what she knows is going on . . . but the money helps a lot.

The daughter longs for love and attention from the one person she doesn't have—her father. Suddenly she's growing up; boys are noticing. A handsome guy who hangs out down the block tells her she's beautiful; he can give her a good time. He says he loves her, can make her happy. She basks in the love and attention of a man. Then at fifteen, she discovers she's pregnant. The guy cools. "That's your problem, baby; get an abortion." Abortions cost money she doesn't have, and besides, she doesn't feel right about it. Mama yells a lot but sticks with her daughter. Another mouth to feed . . . but a baby is a baby. The daughter drops out of school. Unable to afford prenatal care, the baby boy is born with a low birth weight. Sixteen and a mother; no diploma, no hope for a decent job, a baby to care for. She goes on welfare.

The baby boy grows up with a mama and a grandma, no man in the house—at least, no man who stays very long. What will change things for him? He can't compete with middle-class society for jobs; he has no role models that suggest he could become a lawyer or teacher or dentist. But, hey, he can become a *man;* he can make babies. He gets a girl pregnant when he's seventeen. By the time he's twenty, he has four children—all by different girls. He stops in to see them once in a while, and brags about his prowess to his friends. "Hey, I'm a daddy four times!" He doesn't contribute to their support. He's following the only path he knows: hanging out, looking out for number one, finding comfort and pleasure in drinking, girls, a little dope. He pulls a few jobs to get survival money—a mom-and-pop grocery, a gas station. One night he's unlucky and gets arrested. Unfortunately, he has a gun, something he carries "for protection." At age twenty-two—when most white youths are graduating from college and landing that first important job—he is in prison.

If even one family were caught in this vicious cycle, it would be cause for concern. But in 1986, over 2 million black families had no member with a secure niche in the work force, what the U.S. Bureau of Census calls the "non-working poor." The media calls them the emerging black underclass. Whatever they are called, most of these families are at risk.

Obviously, the crisis in the family is not limited to the black community, or even the poor. Fatherless children, pregnant teenagers, divorce, drugs, AIDS, child abuse, abortion—these tragedies cut across all economic levels, races, and classes in America. Other social forces are at work: permissive attitudes toward sexuality; scorn for religious values; a breakdown in community; and an increase in individualism and materialism. But coupled with a long history of racism and poverty, the impact on the black family in particular is devastating.

Let's look further at some of the issues affecting today's African-American families.

### Loss of Our Spiritual Freedom

First and foremost, we have a crisis in the black family because we have gotten away from biblical principles. Families no longer read the Bible together, and many don't go to church. The name of Jesus has become nothing more than a swear word. Instead of doing the right thing according to the Word of God, each person simply looks out for number one. Most don't have any worthy standards; they don't have any rules to go by.

This void has allowed secular humanism, a godless philosophy which is spreading across the country, to invade our homes, schools, communities, and churches. This has helped create a problem for all American families, especially black families.

Remember the story about the frog and the hot water? If you put a frog in hot water, it will immediately jump out. But if you put the same frog in cool water and gradually increase the temperature, the frog will sit there blinking its eyes happily while it stews to death.

Without the foundation of the Word of God, the standards and morals in our society have been gradually slipping away, until we are in a state of danger that most don't even seem to notice. But the effects of "turning up the heat" of moral decay are destroying our families and crippling the next generation.

Even when children are taught values at home, they go to school where teachers don't believe in or aren't (or think they aren't) allowed to teach Judeo-Christian principles. The fact that the Pilgrims came to America seeking religious freedom has been deleted from some history books; the role that Christianity has played in many of the great reform movements is ignored; even the work of Dr. Martin Luther King, Jr. and other black leaders is not honored by some, or is seen as insignificant. (Fortunately, the great hue and cry by some Christian leaders about some of these imbalanced views is pressing some textbook publishers to reconsider.)

Solid values of right and wrong have been replaced with so-called "neutral values." When fifth-grade children report that they can't talk about God at their school because they'll get in trouble, they have been powerfully intimidated by a very sad value system. Because of the permissiveness that's allowed in the schools, peer pressure is stronger on our children than adult authority. Even the church has failed to be a bulwark against the eroding values of our day. Too many church members—and ministers too—

say one thing on Sunday and live another the rest of the week.

The sad thing is that historically a strong spiritual foundation has helped the black family—and thus us as a people—survive decades and centuries of difficult challenges.

The effect of changing values jolted Wanda and me when we returned to the States in 1964 from Monrovia, Liberia, where we had lived for six years at radio station ELWA, a beautiful location along the coast of the Atlantic Ocean. As a family we produced radio programs, and I frequently conducted evangelistic crusades throughout Liberia and other countries in Africa. These various ministries were under the auspices of the Billy Graham Evangelistic Association.

In a sense, our children had lived a sheltered life in Africa. But back in New York and then in Ohio, they struggled with what they perceived to be our old-fashioned rules and what "all the other kids" were doing. When we told them they had to be in at a certain hour, they resisted at times. Many of their friends had no curfews. As we became aware of various families' situations, some of these homes seemed stable enough (the father was present and providing for the family), but there were no established standards. And some kids came from homes where the father—and sometimes the mother—was an alcoholic.

Even though we felt under a lot of pressure, we continued to build our family life on the Word of God, with daily Bible reading and prayer. We wanted to know who our children's friends were, what they were doing, and when they'd be home. We encouraged involvement with church activities and youth events. Alcohol, profanity, and questionable literature had no place in our home.

One boy told our girls, "You know, you're blessed to have such a family. I wish I had a family like that. My old man doesn't care." This boy, who was not a Christian, could see the benefits of a Christian family.

Our three oldest girls had been singing together for several years. Everyone knew them as the Jones Sisters Trio, recording artists, who sang in Billy Graham crusades, and appeared on the "Day of Discovery" TV programs. During this time a young man said, "Cheryl, Gail, Phyllis . . . look, please don't mess up, because everybody is waiting for the Jones sisters to fall." The girls didn't realize that other young people were watching their conduct as Christians. It was a little scary, but in a way it was good for them too.

From our experience in counseling families, we know a lot of kids may rebel, but deep down in their hearts they would like to have someone say no to them when they head in a wrong direction. Setting limits can show children that they are loved and cared for. They want to know that Someone is in control of the universe, because their own lives often feel out of control. They want purpose and meaning in their lives, the kind of purpose that can only come through a personal relationship with Jesus Christ. When this spiritual foundation is missing, the family has no center on which to build, no guiding map to chart its path through the troubling waters of our times.

## Breakdown of the Traditional Family

Hand in hand with the loss of our spiritual foundation is the breakdown of the traditional family. When we say the "traditional" family, we mean it in the sense of the biblical structure where a husband and wife are legally married and are responsible for the children who result from this union. Some would define traditional family too narrowly—with only the father as breadwinner and the mother as homemaker. But given the historical role of the black family (which often includes extended family members or substitute parents) and economic pressures (which often means that more than one adult must work to support the family), we feel there are variations of family that nonetheless are rooted in the biblical concept: husband and wife, committing themselves before God, with the support of family and church, to create a new family unit.

Unfortunately, the concept of "family" is being stretched today to include all sorts of aberrations. *Newsweek's* special on the family (Winter/Spring 1990), for instance, included examples of gay and lesbian partners raising children, giving them unprecedented new "respectability." The primary problem in the breakdown of the family, however, is that both men and women have been avoiding or abandoning marriage in record numbers in recent years. According to the University of Maryland's Dr. Andrew Billingsley, "This behavior constitutes the leading edge of the contemporary black family crisis."[1]

This is a fairly recent phenomenon. As late as 1960, 78 percent of all black families with children were headed by married couples. The rapid decline of two-parent families in the black community in the last thirty years can be seen in the following statistics:[2]

1960: 78 percent of black families with children were headed by married couples.
1970: Only 64 percent were headed by married couples.
1975: Only 54 percent.
1980: Only 48 percent.
1985: Only 40 percent.
1990: Only 37 percent (estimated).

Or to put it another way, in 1960 only 22 percent of black families had only one parent in the home. But in 1980 single-parent families *outnumbered* two-parent families for the first time. In 1990 the number of single-parent families had jumped to 63 percent.

Although many of these statistics include families disrupted by divorce, an alarming number did not include marriage at all. At the end of the '80s, more than half of all black babies were born out of wedlock.[3] And 60 percent of all black families had no father in the home.

This is indeed alarming. First, children in black, female-

headed families are five times as likely to be on welfare
than those in intact black families.[4] More often than not
this means poor health care, substandard housing, inferior
education resulting in poor motivation, dependence on
welfare, unemployment. Second, "the predicament of fe-
male-headed households feeds on itself because boys (and
girls) raised in such families may have no role model for
marriage and fatherhood."[5] The consequences of growing
up fatherless are just beginning to be understood by those
concerned about the family. Cornell's Urie Bronfenbren-
ner has linked "father absence" to many problems common among black youths in the inner city, such as "low
motivation for achievement, inability to defer immediate
rewards for later benefits, low self-esteem, susceptibility to
group influence . . . and juvenile delinquency."[6]

Dr. Louis Sullivan, U.S. Secretary of Human Services,
wrote a provocative article in *USA Today,* June 14, 1991
entilted "Time to Get Dads Back into U.S. Families." Note
a portion of what he said:

> Too many American fathers have decided it is too
> rough for them to handle. So literally millions of our
> nation's children—rich and poor alike—live with the
> anger, loneliness, and insecurity produced by absen-
> tee fathers.
>
> Some of the fathers have neglected to form a family
> in the first place—households headed by a single
> mother have *doubled* since 1960. In other instances,
> divorce, separation, neglect, abandonment, or work-
> aholism deprive children of their fathers.
>
> It is well understood that father absence is com-
> mon among the poor. Often overlooked is that many
> children of our middle and wealthy classes experi-
> ence the problem also—not from a poverty of means,
> but from a poverty of parenting. They have material
> advantages, but many are suffering emotional depri-
> vation and actual neglect. . . .

It is not acceptable when fathers abandon their children, either in fact or in attitude. The father who acts more attached to his golf game or his TV program than to his children needs to rethink his priorities. And we certainly cannot stand idly by while the negative father-substitutes—drug kings, gang leaders and other insincere, false roleplayers—prey on our vulnerable youth.

We must work to get our fathers back into our American families. At the same time, it is vitally important for caring adults to be father substitutes where families have not been established or cannot be restored. Through mentoring relationships we can instill important values and teach accountability to youngsters who are at risk.

Through our combined efforts, we can weave a new social climate where children will be nurtured, where adolescents will be guided and cared for and where our young people will be prepared for adulthood by giving them equal measures of love, discipline, challenge, and responsibility.

This is not an indictment against single women and mothers, many of whom are struggling valiantly against overwhelming odds to bring up their children. It is an indictment against our political priorities that pours more money into weapons than into job training and opportunities. It is an indictment against our society's pervasive permissiveness of sexual activity apart from marriage and general negligence of stressing the importance of the father role. It is also an indictment against the church and Christian community that among our own members and families we have failed to teach and communicate God's idea for marriage, committed and faithful sexual relationships between men and women, and the importance of the family in nurturing, caring for, and training our young.

Some people are actually saying, "We don't need the

family. The whole idea of marriage and the family is for the birds. You do what you want to do. We'll do our own thing." This attitude has led to promiscuous sex, couples just living or shacking up together, serial partners, artificial insemination of single women, or couples choosing careers, wealth, and freedom over the responsibilities of parenthood. Probably the most devastating result of this libertarian attitude is the millions of babies who have been aborted, and the millions more who are growing up without the benefit of married parents who are committed to each other and their children in love.

We want to lift our voice in defense of the traditional family because there are many anti-Christian forces working to destroy it. This is where we stand, because God's Word does not change. Jesus told the Pharisees that it was only because of the hardness of people's hearts that Moses' Law permitted divorce. "But," He said, "at the beginning of creation God 'made them male and female.' 'For this reason a man will leave his father and mother and be united to his wife, and the two will become one flesh.' So they are no longer two, but one. Therefore what God has joined together, let man not separate" (Mark 10:6-9).

God hasn't changed His mind about marriage, and He had a pretty good idea to start with. He created us for marriage, commitment, faithfulness, and love. This has been and always will be the core of a strong family, and we're happy to find happy African-American Christian families across the country.

## Children Having Children

In discussing the effects of poverty on the family, we come to a major concern in our community: children having children. Teen pregnancy is a leading cause of poverty among African Americans. At their age, these young mothers are undereducated and lack job skills. The fathers, also, are not prepared to take on the responsibilities of supporting a family. Though welfare kicks in to support mother and child, it perpetuates a vicious cycle.

What are some of the causes of this epidemic of teen pregnancy? Some might place the whole blame on the general hopeless condition of the black underclass. Poverty, unemployment, racism—these certainly take their toll. But, says Georgia L. McMurray, president of a New York consulting firm and visiting professor in social policy at Fordham University, "Among African-Americans, 'hard times' is not a new phenomenon. What is new is the change in expectations for personal responsibility, not only in black culture, but also in the U.S. society as a whole. Moreover, *the destigmatization of premarital sex and bearing children without marriage may have as equally devastating an effect as the lack of a good job,* of whether to marry, even to be responsible for the consequences of sexual activity [italics added].

"Based upon several studies, certain at-risk groups among adolescents can be pinpointed," McMurray continues. "For example, girls who have school problems—poor achievement, poor discipline, truancy—and whose families receive public assistance tend to be at highest risk of pregnancy. This seems to hold true of males as well." An additional critical factor is that black youths, like their white counterparts, "seem to be cultivating new and perhaps libertarian views towards sexual activity and personal responsibility that do not augur well for the future development of black families." Studies have also shown that "girls willing to entertain the idea of pregnancy were two to three times more likely to bear a child."[7]

Christian parents, pastors, and educators, sit up and listen! What greater challenge do we need to lift up the vision of sexual abstinence until marriage (i.e., true sexual responsibility)? This is one of the great weaknesses of the approach to sex education so prevalent in our public schools where the attitude often is: "We hope you delay sexual activity, but if you are sexually active, be 'responsible' and practice 'safe sex' " (i.e., use contraceptives). The contraceptive message is not stemming the tide óf teenage pregnancies in our nation. The Alan Guttmacher Institute (formerly the research arm of Planned Parenthood) originally estimated that there would be two to three hundred fewer pregnancies per thousand clients served by school-based clinics dispensing contraceptives to teenagers. Instead, researchers writing for the *Wall Street Journal* found that as the number of teenage clients increased, there were fifty to one hundred *more* pregnancies per thousand clients.[8] When expectations are that "everybody is doing it" and "responsible sex" is equated with using condoms, teenagers who might choose to wait feel more and more isolated and alone.

What is needed is a change in attitude, a change in the heart. We need to celebrate God's idea for sex: He created it, it is right, it is good—in the context of committed, married love, between a man and a woman capable of caring for any children created as a result of the union. Yes, let's tell our young people that sex is great! But like all good things, it can be used as a gift of God . . . or abused. And those who suffer most are the children, born to parents who are barely more than children themselves.

Some of the studies mentioned by Georgia McMurray have also explored inhibiting factors on teenage pregnancy—those influences that help teenagers say no to premarital sex. What are these factors? (1) *Close parental supervision*, (2) *a high-quality relationship with their parents*, and (3) *religion*. Also, teenagers who want to go to college and plan ahead for their future tend to have dramatically lower birthrates. Setting goals, looking to the future, being aware of opportunities for further education, training, and jobs are all positive steps for young people.

This is important. This is something we parents and Christian adults in the black community can do for our own children. Of course, economics and racism and social mores impact our kids. But we can't sit around waiting for the world to change. We have to begin where we are—with our own children in our own homes and churches.

A word of hope and caution: though the risk factors are greatly increased, teen pregnancy does not have to be a dead end. Counseling for the teenagers (the teenage mother *and* father) and their parents can help them work through many of the emotional stresses and decisions that need to be made. Direct intervention programs which assist teen parents in health care for their child, parenting skills, child care, finishing high school, and developing job skills can greatly reduce the number of teen parents who permanently end up as part of the underclass.

**The Plight of the African-American Male**
"It ain't easy being green," sings Kermit the Frog, but it's a lot easier than being a black male in these days. For instance:

- There are well over 3 million black men who either can't find work or are working and not making enough money to sustain a family.[9]
- The leading cause of death of black males between the ages of fifteen and twenty-four is homicide.[10] And they are ten times more likely to be murder victims than whites.[11]
- Nationwide, black men represent 46 percent of state prison inmates but only 6 percent of the U.S. population.[12] (All blacks comprise 11 percent of the population.)
- Among black men who are in their twenties, 23 percent are incarcerated or on probation or parole.[13]
- In the ten largest urban cities, the high school dropout rate for black males is 72 percent.[14]
- Only 2.7 percent of African-American men attend a four-year college.[15]

These sad statistics—and possibly the fact that black

men have a lower life expectancy than their white counter-parts—have led one social scientist to estimate that there is only one *available* black male per five unmarried black females. The result is that about 47 percent of black families currently are single-parent homes headed by women in contrast to the 1880s when 84 percent of rural black families and 72 percent of urban black families were father-headed households.[16]

How we respond to these problems will be the test for us as men. Dr. Nelson Onyenwok, of the Center for the Study of the Black Male at Albany State College in Georgia, says, "We intend to counter the things that are being written and said about black men. . . . Reciting negative statistics does not encourage us."[17] True, it's not very encouraging, but the solution must be more than objecting to the statistics because they don't make us feel good. We must change the facts!

The obvious question is, how have we come to this sad condition? Here are a few possible causes.

● *Unemployment, the welfare system and loss of self-esteem.* We have already mentioned the effect of unemployment and the welfare system on the whole family, but it has a special impact on African-American men. Cleveland Municipal Court Judge Ron Adrine says that "a lot of black men . . . feel that they have no legitimate hope of ever achieving the American Dream. Therefore, they have selected not to run the rat race, because they start off on the losing end."[18]

● *The notion that fathering children is a symbol of male prowess.* With much of what it means to be a man in America seemingly unattainable to the black underclass, young black men prove their manhood however they can—regardless of the consequences. John Denson, ex-offender, says that in his neighborhood, "you wasn't a man until you got arrested. We looked forward to it."[19] For others it is alcohol or drugs or gang affiliation. But the most common rite of manhood is "making babies."

The Rev. Ron Williams, pastor of the Church of the Brethren, Cleveland, Ohio, says, "Many of our young people regardless of race or background have no direction, correction, or purpose in their lives, and I believe much of the fault lies with men who want to father children but not be a father to them. . . . As long as boys and girls and men and women want the thrill of intimacy but not the responsibility for the results of their actions, abortion clinics will continue to thrive, and those children that are born will continue to have to do the best they can, raising themselves."[20]

• *The inadequate number of positive male role models.* Dr. Spencer H. Holland, director of the Center for Educating African-American Males at Morgan State University in Baltimore, claims that "women raise sons, not men." And because of the absence of positive male role models in the lives of many black boys, Holland charts what he considers is a human tragedy. Young black boys begin school eagerly, but by the time they are in the fourth grade, they shut down. Holland says, "Only an African-American male can teach an African-American boy what it means to be an African-American man. A white man can help, but women can't do the job."[21] Therefore, Holland has started Project 2000 in which he recruits black men not only to teach but to work on a volunteer basis with young black boys in the classroom. Holland says, "It is unreasonable to expect African-American boys to want to become doctors, lawyers, or Indian chiefs if there aren't any around them."[22]

• *Failure of society to stress the importance of the father's role.* Socially we are caught in a bind between upholding the model of the two-parent family and the necessity of supporting and encouraging single parents in their situation. "We know that children need intact families that include fathers, but we fear to say it lest we appear to be blaming hard-pressed single mothers for the very problems they are struggling to overcome."[23]

Author and social scientist George Gilder has said that "only fathers can support families, reliably discipline teenage boys, and lift a community from poverty. The idea that current welfare mothers can do it while the government raises their children is incredibly naive."[24] And yet many single mothers, struggling valiantly to keep their families together, resent any implication that their efforts aren't good enough. Though the feeling is understandable, men pick up the not-so-hidden message: that they aren't needed.

This message is reinforced by radical elements in the feminist movement (primarily among white feminists). If men and women are really the same (except for a few biological differences), if a woman can do everything a man can do, why does a woman need a man in the home? This is not to negate some of the important gains won by the women's movement. A lot of false stereotypes have been rightly dispelled in recent years. It is good that the workplace has been opened to women, and it is good that men have been encouraged to be more involved with their children at home. But what has suffered is the definition of a husband's and father's role in the family with sufficient distinction and importance to keep him from walking off.

Some women who have been abused by fathers, brothers, or uncles or abandoned by partners fail to establish healthy relationships with men. Children growing up in such a male-hostile environment pick up the message that a father in the home is not essential or even desirable, and they are much more likely to duplicate the single-parent model.

In his book *Biblical Faith and Fathering,* John Miller points out how tenuous the father's role is in the family. For the nine months of pregnancy, during the travail of birth itself, and during the first period of life after birth, the mother is absolutely essential. In all this, she bonds with the child and the child with her, and there is never

**61**

any question about who the mother is. But the same is not true for the father. After impregnation, his presence is not physically required. In fact, unless the mother is faithful and truthful, there is no obvious certainty who the father is.[25] His importance to the family is much more emotional and spiritual, and that can be very easily upset if he is denied a place of significance in the family.

Lest we despair of the plight of the African-American male, we need to remember: most black men are *not* in prison, they are *not* drug dealers, they are *not* homosexuals, they have *not* left their families, and they are employed. But we would do well to listen to columnist William Raspberry who wrote:

> If I could offer a single prescription for the survival of America, and particularly of black America, it would be: restore the family.
>
> And if you asked me how to do it, my answer—doubtless oversimplified—would be: save the boys. . . .
>
> We can't rescue America's families unless we make up our minds to save the boys.[26]

**Some things to think about and do:**
1. Which of the issues mentioned in this chapter—loss of our spiritual foundation, breakdown of the traditional family structure, children having children, plight of the black male—come closest to home for you in defining the crisis points in your own life and family?
2. If you are a black male, who have been your role models as to what it means to be a man, and what has their example taught you?
3. What do you think William Raspberry means when he says a critical ingredient in restoring the black family is to "save the boys"? Do you agree or disagree?

## - 5 -
## Rebuilding the Foundation

*Lord, lift me up and let me stand,*
*By faith, on heaven's tableland;*
*A higher plane than I have found;*
*Lord, plant my feet on higher ground.*
J o h n s o n  O a t m a n ,  J r .

**On Family Night** in one of our evangelistic crusades in New England, I gave a message on how to establish a happy marriage and home. For my text I read Joshua 24:15:

> But if serving the Lord seems undesirable to you, then choose for yourselves this day whom you will serve, whether the gods your forefathers served beyond the River, or the gods of the Amorites, in whose land you are living. *But as for me and my household, we will serve the Lord.* (Emphasis added.)

I challenged the audience to make Christ the head of their homes, to evaluate what was happening in their marriages—with their children, how they were handling money, and the priorities in their lives—by the guiding principles of Scripture. Were husband and wife having difficulties? Were the kids disrespectful and unmanageable? Did they feel like giving up? I emphasized that it wasn't too late to get down on their knees and give their lives and families to God. It wasn't too late to rebuild their homes on Christ, the only solid foundation that can withstand the pressures and temptations coming at the family from every side.

Then I gave the invitation. Many came forward. Later in the counseling room, a counselor brought a couple to me and said, "I think you might like to talk with these folks, Dr. Jones."

The man had tears streaming down his face. But he told this story:

> My wife and I have been separated for many years. Our home life was so bad that the city came and took away our children, who are now living in foster homes. We saw no hope for our marriage, so we have recently filed for divorce. But the other day a friend of mine invited me to your crusade. I was feeling so hopeless I thought, "Why not?" Unknown to me, another mutual friend invited my wife.
>
> When you preached on marriage tonight, something happened, and I believe it's the work of God. I came forward and prayed to receive Christ as my Savior. I'd made such a mess of my life, I wanted to give my life to God and let Him take over. Then, I saw my wife in the counseling room! I didn't even know she was here tonight! But she also came forward to give her life to Christ.

I noticed that the wife too was crying. They were holding hands.

The husband looked at his wife and said, "Now that we've both given ourselves to Christ, we want to give up our plans for divorce and start our marriage over again — this time with Christ at the center."

What a time of joy we had! We all prayed and hugged and cried together. As they left that auditorium, the man said, "Dr. Jones, we're going to pray that God will give us our children back, so that we can have a complete home with Christ at the head."

Our international "Hour of Freedom" broadcast, aired on a weekly basis, helps and encourages people. One Christian wife wrote, "I've prayed much for my unsaved husband, an alcoholic. While listening to your radio sermon, he received Jesus Christ as Savior. He's a new man, and we're happy as a family."

Beyond the troubling statistics in the last two chapters are the very human stories like these two couples who stood on the brink of disaster, except for the grace of God. The state of the family is eroding at such an alarming rate that the media has been sitting up and taking notice. A series on the "state of the black family" was aired on the black entertainment network in our area on a daily TV program called *Our Voices*. On one of these programs, host Bev Smith asked, "What can we do to restore the black family?"

This is the question we would like to address.

## Rebuild the Spiritual Foundation

Many families are in trouble because the foundation is weak. If we want to restore the family, we must begin by laying a strong spiritual foundation. The Word of God says, "Unless the Lord builds the house, its builders labor in vain" (Ps. 127:1).

Jesus told a parable (Matt. 7:24-27) about a man who dug deep and built his house upon solid rock. When the storms came it stood because it had a solid foundation. Another man built his house on sand. It may have been a beautiful house; but when it was buffeted by storms, it simply collapsed—no strong foundation. Jesus said this is what happens when someone hears His words but doesn't put them into practice.

You cannot build a good family on materialism or pleasure. You cannot build a good family on alcohol and drug abuse. You cannot sneer at values like integrity, honesty, hard work, respect for parents, and love of neighbor and hope to build a good family. You cannot provide what your children really need if you fail to build on a foundation that holds in the hard times as well as the sunny days.

The Bible has a lot to say about this foundation. *First of all, a firm foundation for the family is one where Jesus Christ is welcomed as Savior and Lord.* This is an individual decision, just as it was for the husband and wife who came to the crusade on the brink of divorce. When they left that meeting, their troubles weren't over; they had some struggles to face. But they had planted their feet on the solid Rock, a saving relationship with Jesus. They had taken the first step in a new direction.

But what happens if you are a believer and your spouse is not? God can work through you to create a Christian home and win your spouse through prayer and your respectful and loving behavior. But if you are a young person, or a single parent or adult, we strongly caution against marrying an unbeliever. The Bible instructs:

> Do not be yoked together with unbelievers. For what do righteousness and wickedness have in common? Or what fellowship can light have with darkness? What harmony is there between Christ and Belial? What does a believer have in common with an unbeliever? (2 Cor. 6:14-15)

After our oldest daughter, Cheryl, married Norman Sanders, a staff member at the Billy Graham Training Center in Asheville, North Carolina, one of our other daughters, Gail, an airline flight attendant, came home for a visit.

I could tell she was quite upset about something. I said, "Gail, what's the trouble?"

She sighed. "Dad, I want to level with you. There's a very fine young man who is a flight attendant. We've had a few dates, and he's a gentleman in every way. He's really going places with the airlines. You know, Cheryl was blessed to get married so soon to Norman, who is a Christian." Then Gail went on to say that she and her sister, Phyllis, also a flight attendant, hadn't found anyone. She fidgeted a little and I waited. "What I'm coming to is, the other girls on the airlines say, 'Gail, you better nail this guy; you don't find fellows like him anymore.' Now, Dad, do you think it would work? He goes to church."

I said, "Gail, is he saved? Does he know the Lord? You know what we believe."

She said, "No."

As gently as I could I told her she had two choices. "You could marry him, but if you marry him, you know God's Word says not to be 'yoked together' with unbelievers. This isn't because he's 'bad,' but you would be pulling in different directions. Or you could say no and tell the Lord you're willing to wait for the man He has in mind for you."

She looked at me and smiled. "Dad, I thought you'd say that. I just needed reassurance." So we sat there at the table and held hands and prayed that God in His time and according to His will and Word would bring the right husbands to her and Phyllis. And in time God answered prayer and two fine Christian professional baseball players with the Cleveland Indians came along. Gail married Andre Thornton, who is now the president of Christian Family Outreach, Inc., Cleveland. Months later Phyllis married Pat Kelly, now an evangelist with Lifeline Ministries in Baltimore.

*Second, a firm foundation for the family is one where Jesus Christ is worshiped as Lord.* By this we mean a home where the Word of God is read and the family prays together regularly. A family's spiritual life shouldn't be limited to going to church on Sunday. The Lord gives some amazing instructions about family life in this regard:

> Be careful, or you will be enticed to turn away and worship other gods. . . . Fix these words of Mine in your hearts and minds; tie them as symbols on your hands and bind them on your foreheads. Teach them to your children, talking about them when you sit at home and when you walk along the road, when you lie down and when you get up. Write them on the doorframes of your houses and on your gates, so that your days and the days of your children may be many (Deut. 11:16, 18-21).

In other words, God's Word should be woven into all areas of family life. This means reading it with your spouse, reading it with your children, and talking about what God says.

Wanda and I have prayer and Bible reading each day and evening. This is aside from time spent separately before the Lord. When I am away in meetings, I frequently call her and we close our conversations in prayer. When our children were home, we also had family devotions together, letting them take turns reading and discussing the Bible, followed by a time of prayer.

This doesn't mean forcing your preschoolers to sit through the "begats" in the Old Testament. You can begin with a Bible story at bedtime; then as your children get older, read some of the exciting stories right from the Bible. As they move into their teen years, read a short passage—five to ten verses—and discuss it together.

Now that our children have left the nest, Wanda and I welcome their visits and the occasions to visit them. We enjoy having fun times and also family devotions together in their homes. Occasionally, they will phone and share prayer requests with us and we with them.

Unfortunately, a lot of families have let prayer and Bible

reading as a family slip by the wayside. There is a story about a pastor who became concerned about a family who had stopped coming to church. So he called to arrange a visit. When he arrived, the family was all dressed up and graciously invited him in. The father said, "Pastor, we're sorry that we haven't been out to church; we just haven't been able to make it. But we want you to know that we've been thinking about you and the members of the church." The father then turned to his young boy. "Son, our pastor is here, and I want you to go and bring us the book we so dearly love as a family." The little boy scampered off and returned shortly with the Sears-Roebuck catalog!

It's become a cliché, but there's real truth in the saying, "The family that prays together, stays together." First of all, prayer acknowledges that we can't build a family alone; we need God's help. We turn to Him day in and day out to ask His guidance for the challenges of family life. And He has promised to help us. Secondly, it's hard to fight and be angry at each other while you're praying together.

When we celebrated our fortieth wedding anniversary several years ago, our children planned a big celebration. They told lots of stories and family secrets on us—stories like the time Wanda ate a whole plate of Christmas cookies that Lisa had carefully decorated, and the not-so-expert haircuts I used to give David in Liberia! But we were moved when one after another of our children shared memories like these: "I'll always remember coming home from school and seeing Dad on his knees praying for us." "Sometimes there would be all-night prayer meetings in our church." "One of my earliest memories is walking into Mom and Dad's room early in the morning and hearing them praying for us." "Now that I'm out on my own, I gain strength from knowing my parents are home praying for me."[1]

Is there friction, tension in the home? Get together and

pray. Ask God to help you love and forgive one another and to show you another way. Pray with your children about the tough times they're experiencing at school or with their friends. Pray with your spouse about how to relate to each other in love. Pray for your friends, your church, your work, your nation. Your family will benefit, and your children will remember.

*Third, a firm foundation is one where Jesus Christ is the head of the family.* In other words, the family not only reads God's Word, but *applies* it to their lives. Jesus sets the standards for the home. A Christian family doesn't try to "keep up with the Joneses" (we've always disliked that phrase—for obvious reasons!). A Christian family doesn't let current fads and attitudes dictate their decisions, but lets God set their priorities.

I recall an experience in our home in Cleveland when one day my dad sat Clarence and me down and said, "There are certain kids who come in this community that I don't want to see you with. They have a bad reputation." I found out later he was right. My parents were very cautious about our friends. They knew that the wrong associations can pull you down, make you compromise your standards, and get you into trouble.

Some parents today seemingly don't care what their kids do; many others care but act helpless to guide their children in the right path. If parents are going to successfully teach and apply godly principles in their home, these principles must be taught in love. We can be firm and loving at the same time. Children may often rebel when limits are set on their behavior, but we must be prepared for this and respond in love without letting down our standards. And also children must also see these principles at work in their parents' lives. You can't tell your daughter to be honest if she sees you telling "little white lies" or being dishonest. You can't tell your son to be pure and chaste if he knows that Dad is not loyal and faithful to Mother. We parents must "walk our talk."

*Fourth, a firm foundation for the family results when husband and wife fulfill their God-given responsibilities to each other according to the Word of God.* That is, the husband is truly the kind of husband and father God intends him to be; the wife is the kind of wife and mother that God intends her to be. This is an area of great confusion today. Men don't know what is expected of them; women are pulled in conflicting directions between homes and careers. There is a great deal of hostility and disrespect between men and women. Both men and women are walking out on family responsibilities to find "personal fulfillment"—or simply because they can't cope.

More about this in the next chapter, but at this point it is enough to say how important it is to build our relationships as husbands and wives on the foundation of God's Word. Not what we *think* the Bible says; not lifting one phrase here or there out of context. But we must study it and see what God has to say. After all, creating man and woman for each other was God's idea in the first place. They were *both* made in the image of God and "it was very good." God's principles, lived with love and grace, are good for both husband and wife.

We say *"rebuild* the spiritual foundation" of the family because it was the Word of God which helped many blacks survive the devastating years of slavery. Our ancestors had a shared faith which held them together. The Gospel gave them hope when all looked hopeless; their faith in Jesus Christ the Savior and the love of God kept them "free" in their spirits when their bodies and lives were shackled. Out of the heartache, trials, and persecutions grew the "Negro spirituals"—a rich heritage of music that was a source of their strength in the Lord during those troubled times. Unfortunately, many educated black Americans think it is beneath them to sing those songs today, that they portray a stereotype of another time and place. They don't realize that the spirituals reveal the dynamic Christian faith of our ancestors and present a challenge to us today. I'm delighted that many black churches and college choirs include them in their musical repertoire.

One night Wanda and I enjoyed a special television program called "Spirituals in Concert," recorded in Carnegie Hall to honor the world renowned black opera singer, Marion Anderson. Jessy Norman and Kathleen Battle were the soloists, accompanied by the chorus and orchestra, with James Leving, director. What a moving spiritual experience that was for us! Great Negro spirituals such as "There Is a Balm in Gilead" and "He's Got the Whole World in His Hands" came alive with new meaning.

That evening we recalled other outstanding black American singing groups such as the Fisk Jubilee Singers, the Cleveland Colored Quintet, the Tuskegee Choir, and the famous Wings Over Jordan Choir heard years ago coast to coast on Sundays over CBS radio. Millions of listeners enjoyed the Wings Over Jordan Choir's unique rendition of the spirituals. President Franklin D. Roosevelt invited the choir to sing at the White House. The singers also traveled abroad and disbanded in the '50s. Some time ago former members and friends began a fund which gives college scholarships annually to students with musical talents.

Some African Americans are also saying that Christianity is a white man's religion, that it must be rejected by the black community. "After all," they say, "the Bible was used to justify slavery by the slaveholders." It is true that God's Word has been twisted and misused by many people all through the centuries to justify their own sinfulness; people are still doing it today. But the Bible says, "There is neither Jew nor Greek, slave nor free, male nor female, for you are all one in Christ Jesus" (Gal. 3:28). When Jesus Christ came, He broke the boundaries of nationality and race to proclaim His love for the whole world. "For God so loved *the world,* that He gave His one and only Son, that whoever believes in Him shall not perish but have eternal life" (John 3:16).

Christ is the hope for the whole world. Christ is the

hope for the black family, and all other families. We must rebuild the family on a spiritual foundation, with Christ as the chief cornerstone.

What else must we do to rebuild the foundation of the black family?

## Restore the Sanctity of Marriage

In a newspaper article titled "Why Are Men Going for the 'Lite' Relationship?" the author says, "It isn't clear that the sexual revolution did women any great favor. Traditionally, women have traded sexual intimacy for commitment. The greatest intimacy was intercourse and the greatest commitment was marriage. Ideally, they took place on the same day. But all that has changed."[2]

Our young people are getting very mixed messages today. In the movies and on TV there is very little support for reserving sexual intimacy for marriage. Sexual "freedom" has created an attitude among young men, especially, of: "Why marry? I can have sex without all the responsibilities." The sexual relationship of a man and a woman is a natural, wonderful thing when experienced as part of a holistic relationship: love, commitment, faithfulness, responsibility for children. But now that sex apart from marriage has been accepted by society, marriage itself has become suspect. Kids are growing up with a distorted view, because they aren't convinced that marriage works anyway. "Why bother," they say. "If we break up, we won't have to go through divorce."

Another distortion is that homosexuality is simply an "alternative lifestyle." I heard about a conference on homosexuality held in one of the historic churches in America. The speaker, a practicing homosexual who claimed to be a Christian, argued that the Bible speaks only to the issue of "lust" or promiscuous relationships, not to homosexual activity per se. But this view is creating a lot of confusion among young people. While Christians need to have compassion toward those who struggle with homosexuality, we must not condone something expressly forbidden by Scripture.[3]

A lot of people *are* concerned about the growing numbers of teen pregnancies, teen parents, sexually transmitted diseases (STDs), and especially AIDS, among all segments of our society—black and white, rich and poor. But in many cases the only solutions offered by schools and youth organizations are contraceptive education and availability, and accessibility of abortion—"and your parents don't have to know." Somehow society is turning a blind eye to the source of the problems: removing sexual experience from the place God intended it as His good gift: the marriage relationship between a man and a woman. Our Lord also uses this fact to illustrate the relationship He has with His church (Eph. 5:23-25).

We will never address these problems among our young people, never stem the long-term impact on families, as growing legions of children grow up with only one parent or experience the devastation of divorce, unless we restore the divine pattern established by God:

> The Lord God said, "It is not good for the man to be alone. I will make a helper suitable for him. . . . For this reason a man will leave his father and mother and be united to his wife, and they will become one flesh" (Gen. 2:18, 24).

"Getting married" in and of itself doesn't address the issue. True marriage means *commitment.* When a couple takes their marriage vows, they are making a pledge before God. The longer Wanda and I are married, the more we realize how important that word *commitment* is. No, it's not always easy. Sickness and hard times can put a strain on a family. Learning to communicate with one's spouse in love takes work; there are misunderstandings. We need to learn to forgive each other, and ask forgiveness. This is why having God at the center of our relationship is so important: we turn to Him for grace; His Word teaches the importance of forgiveness, and what it means to love.

In his helpful book called *Hedges—Loving Your Marriage Enough to Protect It,*[4] Jerry Jenkins speaks primarily to men about the sanctity of marriage and the importance of setting "hedges" around their behavior toward other women once they have made a commitment to one woman. His suggestions are practical: Don't flirt, even in jest; if you are a pastor or professional and counsel the opposite sex, have a third person present; keep compliments to female co-workers impersonal ("That's a nice dress," not "You look gorgeous today!"). If we *believe* that marriage is a sacred commitment, it affects the way we behave, the decisions we make, and what our priorities are.

As one fifteen-year-old said to her parents recently, "You don't know how much it means to me to know that you wouldn't even *consider* divorcing each other. I go to sleep at night secure because my family is always going to be there for me." Now that's commitment; that young teen has a model of what a marriage relationship can be that will be a spiritual foundation for her own future.

Many young people are scared of marriage; they don't see models of committed marriages. Most of their friends' parents are divorced, or are on their second or third marriages, or maybe these kids never knew their fathers at all. If all they know is what they see around them today, they won't know what marriage can be.

That's why we as adults in the black community must recommit ourselves to the sanctity of marriage; we must not allow divorce to be an easy out when we have problems. We must once again teach (and model) that sex should be reserved for the marriage relationship, when two people are ready to commit themselves to each other and take responsibility for establishing a new family unit. We must help our children understand that God ordained marriage to protect and provide for the family, so that every member has the love and support to become all that God meant for them to be.

This is a monumental task. But with God all things are possible. We can begin where we are—with ourselves, with our own families, in our own churches. But it will mean each family member—husband, wife, extended family—discovering and reclaiming the role that God has for them in the family.

The next chapter continues discussion of rebuilding some of the most important foundational elements for a strong family.

**Some things to think about and do:**
1. Have you asked Jesus to be Lord and Savior of your life? If not, talk with your pastor or a Christian friend about what this means.
2. If you are married, do you and your spouse regularly read the Bible and pray together with your children? If not, try it for a week; see what happens. Some suggestions for reading: The Gospel of Matthew, the Gospel of John, Romans, Ephesians, 1 John (all in the New Testament).
3. What is your commitment to the sanctity of marriage (i.e., reserving sexual intimacy for your spouse)? If you have broken this commitment, ask God to help you ask forgiveness of those you have wronged, and enable you to live a clean and holy life before your family.

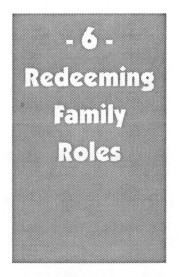

## - 6 -
## Redeeming Family Roles

*Lord, I want to be more loving in my heart, in my heart.*
*Lord, I want to be more loving in my heart, in my heart.*
**Traditional**

**As mentioned earlier,** there is a lot of confusion today about the roles of men and women, especially in marriage. A lot of men are failing because they're listening to the wrong signals; they don't really know what their role is in the family.

### The Role of the Husband

An early slogan in the women's movement touted, "A woman without a man is like a fish without a bicycle." That is, women don't have to depend on men; they're capable themselves. But how does a man hear that message? "Women don't need me; I can do what I want." Too many men have just abdicated their responsibility. They father children to prove their manhood but leave the raising to women. Some are lazy, refusing to work. Some men – angry over the hostility they have experienced – are abusive; this is a very serious problem. Yet the kids are listening to rap groups like Two Live Crew, whose raps advocate violent sex and demean women in the grossest way.

The diminished role of the husband and father in the home is the result of many complex factors, as we explored in chapters 3 and 4. Some men, undereducated and underemployed, feel discouraged; welfare can provide for their families better than they can, so they split. Alcohol, drugs, crime, and the high percentage of blacks in prison are also robbing our homes of the men we so desperately need to help build a new foundation. This is the particular concern of the Nehemiah Family Project in Washington, D.C.

Many years ago I preached a series of revival messages at the Havenscourt Colonial Church in Oakland, California. Unknown to me there was a twelve-year-old boy named Don Lewis who came each night and heard my messages about putting God at the center of our lives and our homes. Today Don Lewis has a burden for the black family. He developed the Nehemiah Family Project to help "rebuild the wall" around the family, much as Nehemiah rebuilt the wall around the ancient city of Jerusalem when it lay in ruins. Don feels the key to rebuilding the family is giving black men a vision for their role of leadership and responsibility to their wives and children. Many have never had a male role model for this task and need retraining from the Word of God.

Tony Evans, pastor of the Oak Cliff Bible Fellowship Church in Dallas, also challenges men regarding their role in the family: "Take back the leadership role," he says.[1] Men shouldn't ask their wives, "May I pretty please be the leader in the home?" Rather, husbands and fathers should begin fulfilling the responsibilities that God has given them and *being* the head of their homes. This may mean asking your wife (or the mother of your children) for for-giveness for leaving the burden of raising the children on her shoulders, for failing to provide leadership for the home. It may mean asking your children for forgiveness for not being there for them when they need you. Some-one has said, "Your children need your presence, not your presents." More often than not, wives will welcome hus-bands willing to take loving leadership for the welfare of the family.

To understand the proper relationship between hus-bands and wives, we need to study Christ's relationship to the church. Here is some food for thought: "If anyone does not provide for his relatives, and especially for his immediate family, he has denied the faith and is worse than an unbeliever" (1 Tim. 5:8).

This is a primary challenge to husbands today: it is *your* responsibility to provide and care for your family. This does not mean that a wife should never work outside the home. In our economy, it may take two incomes to sup-port the family. Or once the children are raised, a woman may have many years to devote to a career or area of service. But it does mean that the burden of providing for the family should not be on the shoulders of the wife and mother. A husband does great harm to his family if he abandons this essential role or if he squanders the family resources on alcohol, drugs, or gambling, or plunges the family into debt to purchase status symbols such as fancy cars and expensive clothes.

On the other side of this issue, husbands should not feel they have fulfilled their family responsibilities just because they bring home a paycheck. Let's look at what else the Scriptures have to say: "Husbands, love your wives, just as Christ loved the church and gave Himself up for her. . . . In this way husbands ought to love their wives as their own bodies. He who loves his wife loves himself" (Eph. 5:25, 28).

Too many husbands have pounced on verse 23, "For the husband is the head of the wife," and neglect to read any further. But Paul was addressing wives at that point! (We'll come back to that.) The emphasis for husbands is *sacrificial love,* just as Christ loved the church so much that He gave up His own life for her. Unfortunately, some men twist being "head of the family" to mean being lord and master and ruling with an iron hand ("What I say goes!").

What a revolution would happen in our marriages if husbands shed this worldly concept of leadership and instead clothed themselves with Christ's example of *servant leadership!* In preaching on this concept, Tony Evans set up this scenario for husbands: "Husband, come home from work, greet your wife and say, 'Honey, I've come home to serve you!' "[2]

What does that mean? That husbands should do the dishes, bathe the kids, scrub the kitchen floor? Well, it may mean doing some of those things! But what it primarily means is seeing to it that your wife is not overburdened with her responsibilities, doing whatever would be an encouragement to her, considering her needs and desires in what needs to be done and decisions that are made.

Right attitudes should translate into appropriate actions and relationships. Different couples may work out tasks and responsibilities in different ways, but the attitude of the husband should be one of sacrificial self-giving. We feel that any man who does this and takes his role seriously before God, *will* be respected by his wife, and she will love and honor him in return. First Peter 3:7 admonishes, "Husbands, . . . be considerate as you live with your wives, and treat them with respect as the weaker partner and as heirs with you of the gracious gift of life, so that nothing will hinder your prayers."

Note that "weaker" does *not* mean "inferior." After all, both man and woman, created in the image of God, are heirs of the gift of salvation! Peter is simply saying that men, who are generally stronger than women physically, should not take advantage of their wives. Instead, they should take even greater care to respect their wives as partners in life together. And, he adds, this tender care for one's wife is necessary to a healthy prayer life.

It is important that husbands encourage and affirm their wives. It's amazing how many men take their wives for granted. We heard of a husband who was thinking about his wife one day on the job. "I've got a good wife," he thought. "She's faithful, she's kind, she's a good mother." So he decided to do something nice for her and on the way home purchased some flowers. When he came home, he handed her the bouquet with a big kiss. To his astonishment, she burst into tears.

"Oh, John," she wailed, "it's been a terrible day. The kids have been fighting, I burned the supper—and now you come home drunk!" Poor John; he gave too little too late.

In the midst of the family crisis today, we praise God for the husbands who do provide for their families and are faithful to their wives, who do lead their families spiritually and give themselves to their children. Let us pray that the influence of these godly men will spread to our young people and others who so desperately need to recapture the vision of what a Christian husband is.

### Renew the Role of the Wife

Just as we need to renew the vision and high calling of being a husband, we need to renew the vision and high calling of being a wife.

The glorious tribute to a wife in Proverbs 31 is still the best description of a godly woman. Not only was this woman skillful and accomplished, but *"her husband has full confidence in her. . . . She brings him good, not harm, all the days of her life"* (vv. 11-12). This is a great gift to a man, to have a wife who is supportive of his efforts and endeavors, who builds him up and encourages him when he is discouraged, who teaches their children to love and respect him.

All too often women are in competition with men today, especially with two incomes. It's "my money" when it should be "*our* money." Or arguments center around "my rights" rather than seeking the good of the other. These are popular attitudes the Christian woman must resist if she wants to help strengthen and establish her home.

*Proverbs 31:20—"She opens her arms to the poor and extends her hands to the needy."* The ministry of caring and compassion is one of the great gifts of womanhood. Wives must be careful that career ambitions or even a narrow focus on one's own family do not inhibit the gift of hospitality and caring for the needs of others. This is traditionally one of the strengths of the black community, one we must continue to nurture.

*Proverbs 31:25—"She is clothed with strength and dignity."* This is a good description of the black wife and mother throughout our heritage. She has persevered in distressing circumstances, through slavery, segregation, and poverty. Even today, when so many African-American men are unable to get jobs, if it weren't for some of these strong wives and single mothers there wouldn't be a family.

*Proverbs 31:26—"She speaks with wisdom, and faithful instruction is on her tongue."* In growing up in Oberlin, Wanda remembers that her mother always spoke wisely, and her teaching has helped Wanda make important choices about what attitudes she was going to have when confronted with life's challenges.

*Proverbs 31:30—"Charm is deceptive, and beauty is fleeting; but a woman who fears the Lord is to be praised."* The influence of godly women on the African-American family is immeasurable. But it's not easy to make loving God a priority in today's society. Women are inundated with advertising for perfume, clothes, makeup—all with the message that these "make the woman." Of course, men like their wives to be attractive, to take pride in their appearance, and a woman should not neglect these things. But they need to be kept in the right perspective. True beauty is a loving and godly spirit.

A woman who fears the Lord needs to consider the scriptural principles about the relation of wives to husbands. These are not popular topics today in an atmosphere of "women's rights." But we need to consider their meaning: "Submit to one another out of reverence for Christ. Wives, submit to your husbands as to the Lord. For the husband is the head of the wife as Christ is the head of the church" (Eph. 5:21-23).

This teaching grows out of the general admonition for Christians (including both husbands and wives) to *submit to one another* out of reverence for Christ. If we make Christ the center of our homes, if husbands are called to give themselves sacrificially to their wives in the same way that Christ loves the church, then wives are called to support and respect this leadership with their wholehearted participation.

But let's be clear: This kind of submission *doesn't* mean being a doormat, or never having an opinion, or not taking responsibility for decisions about the family. It *does* mean enabling your husband to fulfill his role through encouragement, respect, support, and godly wisdom. It is truly an equal partnership, even though the roles are somewhat different. The Apostle Paul admits that these things are "a profound mystery" (Eph. 5:32), but they reflect the relation of Christ and the church.

Some women say, "Sure, I'd be glad to respect a godly husband who had the welfare of his wife and family as his first priority. But you should see the lout I'm married to!" This is actually a serious question. What does the wife do whose husband is not a Christian, or who doesn't provide for his family properly, or who drinks or is verbally abusive? First let's look at what Scripture says:

> If you suffer for doing good and you endure it, this is commendable before God. . . . Wives, in the same

way be submissive to your husbands so that, if any of them do not believe the word, they may be won over without words by the behavior of their wives, when they see the purity and reverence of your lives. Your beauty should not come from outward adornment . . . . Instead, it should be that of your inner self, the unfading beauty of a gentle and quiet spirit, which is of great worth in God's sight (1 Peter 2:20; 3:1-4).

We must realize first of all that this is a very difficult situation. As a Christian woman, a wife would really have to seek the Lord concerning what her approach to her husband should be. She should read the Scripture and pray, asking God what to do. God promises, "Trust the Lord with all your heart and lean not on your own understanding; in all your ways acknowledge Him and He will make your paths straight [direct your path]" (Prov. 3:5-6). Depending on the circumstances, she might also request support and counsel from her pastor or a Christian counselor. (Obviously, if her husband is physically abusive, she must get help and protection, even if it means leaving him.)

If a wife will pray for her husband and approach him in this way, it is possible for him to turn around. Sometimes it doesn't come all at once, but with God, all things are possible. There isn't any situation too hard for God to redeem if we are faithful.

### Restore the Role of the Extended Family

The extended family has traditionally been an important strength of the black family. In years past there were no rest homes, and there was usually an elderly aunt or grandparent in the home, helping to care for the children and passing on years of experience and wisdom. Even if there was an "old folks home" in which to put the older members, most people said, "No, they belong to us; we're going to keep them as long as we can." This is a carryover from our African heritage, where there was a family loyalty that reverences older people, gives them a place of respect, and that includes aunts and uncles and other older family members.

When we lived in Liberia, a man named Robert used to do some work for us. I noticed that his shoes were just about worn out. I had an extra pair I thought might fit, so I gave them to him. Robert was very pleased and showed the shoes around to everyone he met. For two Sundays he showed up at church wearing his new shoes, but the third Sunday he was wearing his old worn-out pair.

"Robert," I said, "where are your new shoes?"

"Oh, Pastor Jones," he said, "my older brother came to visit from the country. He wanted to know where I got my shoes, so I told him. He said he wanted the shoes and that I should give them to him because he is the older brother. So I did."

I felt a little irked. "You mean you gave him the shoes that I gave to you?"

"Pastor, that's our custom. If there's a need in the family, they have a right to take what we have because we respect any family member who is older."

That custom may not always be fair, but the attitude is a far cry from the fate of many elderly people today. We have visited many older folks in rest homes and hospitals who never have a visit from their families. It is like they have been discarded. The trend among many young people today is to feel they no longer need the older generation; they know everything and can't be told anything by parents and grandparents who are too "old fashioned." The extended family network is weakening.

In our concern to restore the black family, we also want to strengthen and restore the role of the extended family. Again, let's see what Scripture has to say:

[Jesus] said to them, "You have a fine way of setting aside the commands of God in order to observe your own traditions! For Moses said, 'Honor your father and your mother,' and 'Anyone who curses his father or mother must be put to death.' But you say that if a man says to his father or mother: 'Whatever help you might otherwise have received from me is Corban' (that is, a gift devoted to God), then you no longer let him do anything for his father or mother. Thus you nullify the word of God by your tradition" (Mark 7:9-13).

In other words, Jesus really scolded the religious leaders for telling people they could give money to the church and then tell their elderly parents: "Sorry, there's nothing left for you. I just gave it all to the temple." The message is clear: we have a responsibility to see that our older family members are cared for.

Admittedly, this is often challenging and can be very disruptive. After we returned from Africa, we settled in New York, from where I continued to travel to various countries and around the states conducting evangelistic crusades and other meetings as part of the Billy Graham Team. On my way home from a California crusade, I stopped in Oberlin to see my parents. I was shocked to find my father had leukemia! My mother was in failing health because of the stress of caring for him—which she had cheerfully tried to keep from us in her letters. When I returned home to New York, I told Wanda how troubled I was about my parents and wondered what we should do. I could hardly ask my wife and children to move again, but that is what I was feeling inside.

I discussed the matter with her and we prayed. Wanda decided to go to Oberlin to assess the situation herself. I remained in New York to conduct an evangelistic crusade at the Apollo Theater. The Jones Sisters Trio sang, as did other musical groups.

When Wanda returned, her mind was made up: "There's only one thing to do; we need to move back to Oberlin to care for Mom and Dad Jones. You're the only surviving son; this is our responsibility." So we moved once again, into my parents' home, where we cared for my father and mother.

It wasn't always easy, especially with my mother, a very independent woman who didn't want things changed from the way she was used to. But I will always appreciate Wanda's attitude when she said, "This is *our* family and *our* responsibility." God blessed the decision. Our children were able to have a special relationship with their grandparents they might otherwise have missed.

Wanda has often said that she regrets that both her parents died before any of our children were born. She would have liked them to know the other side of their roots.

Among some families in the black community, the importance of the extended family is being revived. People are taking an interest in having family reunions, bringing several different generations together to pass on the stories and learn from one another. For instance, the nineteen children (and their children and grandchildren) of Reverend Z. and Mrs. Mattie Broadous have been having a family reunion every three years since 1941! They have published four editions of a souvenir book with photos and short biographies of each branch of the family tree. The introduction to the 1985 edition reads in part:

> We (sisters and brothers) have lived to see many changes in our society and the world in general .... In the midst of all of these changes, God has continued to bless and to bring us together, where we can share our experiences, rejoice over our achievements, and encourage each other in our failures. ... [We] thank God for our family. [We] praise Him for our sainted father and mother and for the principles they instilled in us. ... Our parents were not wealthy so they left no worldly goods to be divided among us, but they left us an abundance of

"loving, caring, and sharing" within us. We take pride in that heritage.[3]

The extended family can shore up a weak link in the family. If there is no father in the home, a grandfather or uncle can take a special interest in the children, provide a caring male presence in a child's life, participate in family activities, and provide a role model that may otherwise be lacking. Sometimes this happens naturally; other times it may need an intentional decision based on a vision for family, and what we can do to bind up the wounded among us.

### Some things to think about and do:

1. If you are married, read the Scriptures that have been mentioned in this chapter and discuss them together. Which biblical principles would help strengthen your marriage? Which biblical principles feel threatening? Why?

2. If you have an unbelieving spouse, study 1 Peter 3:1-7. Are you praying for your spouse? Are there things that need to change in your attitude or behavior to be a loving witness toward your spouse? Do you have a pastor or counselor you can talk to about the situation and receive support?

3. If you are unmarried or a single parent, how do you feel these principles for rebuilding the foundation of the family apply to you? What can single parents do to receive support for rebuilding the family in the absence of a spouse?

4. Whether married or unmarried, make a commitment to begin reading God's Word daily, and set aside time for personal and/or family prayer. Try it for two weeks. What has been the effect on you? On your family?

# - 7 -
# Reclaiming Family Values

*I shall not, I shall not be moved.*
*I shall not, I shall not be moved.*
*Just like a tree that's planted by the water*
*I shall not be moved.*
Traditional

**Several years ago** a TV special called "Ethics and Business" took the viewer into a classroom of high schoolers interested in going into business. A hypothetical question was posed to the students: "You're in business making a certain product. Your own research tells you that continuing to produce this product would cause toxic materials to seep into the water supply and in five to seven years would affect the health of the surrounding community—but would also make you a great deal of money. *And* there's almost no chance that you would be caught. Would you go ahead with it?" The majority of students said yes, they would, if there was only a minimal chance of getting caught! And these are future business leaders.

How have we come so far from the basic moral values of honesty, integrity, and the welfare of others? The breakdown in values is infecting not only business ethics, but personal and social ethics as well . . . with obvious consequences for the family. Yet it is in the family that these values must first be taught.

Some black leaders are saying the family can be restored and maintained only if social conditions improve, if blacks have better jobs, if we get out and vote so we can change political policy, etc. Yes, these are important issues; however, we are concerned when even ministers say nothing about the root problem, which is a spiritual one. The cover of the December 17, 1990 issue of *Newsweek* proclaimed, "Young Americans Return to God." Yet the accompanying article was disturbing. It seems that many young Americans are returning to church, but on their own terms: "Singles still consider their private lives off-limits. . . . They have a keen eye for the sins of society, 'but as for individual sin . . . it's kind of lost.' "[1]

Wanda has often said to our children something her mother used to say to her: "You take yourself wherever you go." What we bring to the political process, how we deal with social problems and economic issues, will be no better than the values we uphold in our personal lives.

Part of rebuilding the foundation for the family is instilling strong moral and spiritual values in our children, so they'll know later how to cope with temptations. Many are becoming teenage alcoholics and falling into the trap of crack and cocaine; young men are getting girls pregnant; they are turning to crime, because they're coming from homes with little support and weak values.

Some parents and schools think a "value-neutral" environment should be cultivated, so that children can choose their own values. This is folly; if we fail to teach what is right, we will then teach that anything goes. This leads to social chaos. Wise King Solomon said, "All a man's ways seem right to him, but the Lord weighs the heart. To do what is right and just is more acceptable than sacrifice" (Prov. 21:2-3).

We believe it's important to teach moral values based on an objective standard: the Word of God. As families read the Bible together, they will discover many principles that, if applied, will strengthen the family relationship and how the family relates to society around them.

The Ten Commandments, for instance, is a biblical summary of God's principles for the family and society. Let's take a look at these moral and spiritual values and how applying them will strengthen our families.

1. *"I am the Lord your God. . . . You shall have no other gods before Me" (Ex. 20:2-3).* God wants to be at the center of our families. So often we put other priorities first: climbing the career ladder, pleasure and good times, gaining material wealth and status, even clothes and looking good. We have made gods out of money, ambition, status—or even alcohol, parties, and "getting high." Unfortunately, this is often at the expense of the family. So many families are pulling in different directions or letting other priorities pull them apart. If we take this commandment seriously, we will make our relationship to God first priority, not just for ourselves, but for our family life.

When Wanda told me, "Yes, I love you, but I need to put Christ first in my life," I didn't understand. But when I put Christ first in my own life, I understood. Christ then gave us a direction for our life together. We had a reason outside of ourselves to exist. By making Him Lord of our family, we had Someone to turn to when we didn't agree; we could pray together when we didn't know what to do. The Bible says, "In all your ways acknowledge Him, and He will make your paths straight" (Prov. 3:5-6).

Putting God at the center of the family gives a focus around which all other life directions can be oriented. And any family that has this focus is going to have an extra strength they wouldn't have otherwise.

Without Jesus Christ at the center, we can't follow the other commandments in our own strength; we will be overwhelmed by all the pressures crushing the family.

*2. You shall not make for yourself an idol in the form of anything. . . . You shall not bow down to them or worship them" (Ex. 20:4).* Many people tend to skip over this commandment; they think it refers to pagan images made of wood and stone. But God is referring to anything that we "worship," that has first place in our lives.

There's a story in the Bible (Matt. 19:1-22) about a rich young man who came to Jesus and asked how he could have eternal life. Jesus told him to obey the commandments: do not murder, do not steal, do not commit adultery, etc. The young man said he obeyed all the commandments—what else? So Jesus told him to give away all his possessions and follow Him. The young man turned away; he couldn't part with his money. Money and possessions had first place in his life; they were his "idols," and they kept him from Christ.

Materialism and greed and pleasure are the idols people worship today. We see many families where the parents have had good upbringing; they come from Christian homes, and we wonder, "Why are their families falling apart and their kids having such serious problems?" Yet in Exodus 20, God says He is a jealous God; if people bow down to other gods, he will punish the children for the sins of the parents to the third and fourth generation! This may be part of God's judgment on our society. American culture is focused heavily on materialism; we are crowding God out of our lives.

In one sense children are paying the price; they are suffering the effects of having our priorities in the wrong places. Families fall apart because easy pleasure is more important than hard work, because getting money—sometimes any way they can—is more important than sacrificing for their families. The kids' heroes are rock stars and movie stars and sport stars—many of whom are self-indulgent and live immoral lifestyles.

We need to help our children understand that nothing should replace God in our hearts. But first we have to ask ourselves to what degree *we* are worshiping the idols of money and possessions and pleasure. We must put God first in our lives and be obedient to His way, and then these other things will take their proper place in our families.

3. *"You shall not misuse the name of the Lord your God" (Ex. 20:7).* To a lot of people God and Jesus Christ are nothing more than swear words. How we obey this commandment often reflects whether the first and second commandments have any reality in our lives. If our children hear us using God and Jesus Christ as swear words, they will have very little reason to respect and love God the Father or His Son Jesus Christ.

The same is true in how we speak to each other. If our children hear us using derogatory names ("Stupid!" "Bitch!" "Dummy!" or worse), there will be little respect for each other in the family. And psychologists have discovered that people who suffer from loss of self-esteem were often verbally abused and put down by their parents. Children tend to believe what their parents tell them; if they are characterized as "stupid" or "good for nothing," they will believe that that is true about themselves. The good news is that encouraging words ("You can do it!" "I believe in you.") can help our children develop a healthy sense of self and become caring, responsible adults.

Another aspect of profanity that concerns us is how God's gift of sex has been dragged through the gutter. How can children develop a reverence and respect for sexual intimacy if we include sexual profanity in our talk? What used to be common talk in the Army and Navy has now become common language in school corridors among young children!

Youth evangelist Josh McDowell once heard one of his children use a sexually explicit word. He asked if the child knew what it meant, and the child said no. So Josh used the occasion (these are "teachable moments"!) to tell the child exactly what it meant, how and when it was appropriate to talk about sexual things, and that all aspects of sex and sexuality should be respected as God's gift for married couples.[2]

We must teach our children that how we talk is important; it shows who we really are inside. Jesus said, "For out of the overflow of the heart the mouth speaks. The good man brings evil things out of the evil stored up in him. But I tell you that men will have to give account on the day of judgment for every careless word they have spoken" (Matt. 12:34-36).

We should talk with our children about the profanity in the music they listen to, the movies they see, and books they read. If they continually listen to profanity, they become insensitive to its destructiveness and the attitudes it creates. Be aware of the rock and rap music groups which are offensive and draw the line: "We don't listen to this in our home."

Instead, we must develop reverence and respect, not only for God, but for each other in the family, and show this by how we speak. In this, as in all the other commandments that teach God's values, parents must first be an example to their children.

4. *"Observe the Sabbath day by keeping it holy"* (Ex. 20:8). Many parents wonder what this means for us today. In early years, my brother Clarence and I lived for a time with our grandparents in Oberlin while our parents were in Chicago on business. Our grandparents were godly people and very strict about what we boys did on Sunday. It was a day of rest. We wore our best clothes and went to Sunday School and church. After church we all enjoyed a good dinner and fellowship together. Sunday was the Lord's Day and we were taught to observe it in a manner pleasing to the Lord.

Today many stores are open on Sunday, and families shop for their groceries or work around the house and yard. Or people sleep in, then pack up their families and go to the beach or play golf, attend games or invite the neighbors over and spend the day in fun and eating. They may take a day of rest but with no thought of giving time to worship God.

A mother asked us recently, "What's the bottom line for keeping the Sabbath? Surely we don't have to go back to the days where you hardly dared breathe on Sunday. On the other hand, how do we keep it 'holy'?"

This commandment goes on to say, "Six days you shall labor and do all your work, but the seventh day is the Sabbath to the Lord your God" (Ex. 20:9-10). We are not under the law relating to the Sabbath in every detail, as the Jews were, but the spirit of the law is still vitally important in our Sunday observance. The spirit of this commandment is that we are to set aside a day from our other pursuits to worship the Lord.

"Keeping the Sabbath day holy" means, first of all, worshiping together as a family. Not merely *sending* the children to Sunday School, or Mom and the children going off to church while Dad parks himself on the couch with the Sunday paper, and later watches the games on TV. We mean the whole family attending church together with the people of God. Turning our hearts toward God on the first day of the week is one more way to help us keep our priorities straight, and to make Jesus the center of our family life.

God knew what He was doing when He set aside one day as a "sabbath rest." Just as our days are broken into daylight and nighttime hours, time for work and time for sleep, so our weeks are broken into six days for work and getting things done, and one day to rest, slow down, have a change of pace. God gives us this commandment, not only for His good (to receive our worship), but for *our* good.

Going to church together, having Sunday dinner around the table, not having to jump up and get work done presumes a certain kind of slowed-down time, where the family can talk and spend time together. If parents make this an important priority, it can't help but nourish and strengthen the family.

5. *"Honor your father and your mother as the Lord your God has commanded you, so that you may live long in the land" (Ex. 20:12).* The Apostle Paul quotes this commandment when he speaks directly to children: "Children, obey your parents in the Lord, for this is right. 'Honor your father and mother'—which is the first commandment with a promise—'that it may go well with you and that you may enjoy long life on the earth' " (Eph. 6:1-2).

Most of us parents wave this commandment before our children when we want them to obey. "Children, obey your parents!" But how many of us sit down and explain to our children the promise God gives to those who are obedient? A child who rebels often gets involved in unhealthy behaviors: running away, drinking or drugs, smoking, sexual promiscuity. Natural consequences often follow, many of which can put a young person seriously at risk, not only spiritually, but physically and emotionally.

Pastor John O'Dell in Dexter, Michigan recently gave a series of messages on the family. He believes one of the primary causes of poor self-esteem is the failure to honor parents. "Every time you look in the mirror," he said to his congregation, "you see some reflection of your parents. You may look like your mom; you have traits like your father. And if you hate them, you're going to hate yourself. Until you resolve that hatred toward them and can honor them, accepting them for who they are, you can never be at peace with yourself."

Some time ago a young man came into crusade offices wanting to see Billy Graham. Dr. Graham wasn't available, so I was asked if I could help. The visitor was clean-cut, well-dressed, but seemed obviously distressed.

"I've got a problem," he said bluntly. "If you can't help me, I've decided to buy a gun and blow my brains out."

"O Lord," I prayed silently, "You've got to help me with this young man."

"I come from a wealthy family," he went on. "About fifteen years ago my dad and I had a bitter quarrel over family business. We said some terrible things to each other, and I haven't spoken with my father since and he hasn't tried to contact me.

"Since then I've wished him dead a thousand times. I hated his guts; in fact, I was proud of the fact that I hated him so much. But, Reverend Jones," he continued, "in the last year or so this hate has been consuming me. It's destroying my family life, it's hurting my business. It's eating me alive inside. I want to get rid of it, but I can't. It seems the only way to get rid of it is to kill myself."

I took him into the Scriptures and showed him Jesus, the Christ of love. Only Jesus can take away our sins; His love is greater than all the hate and abuse of the whole world. Christ wants to meet each one of us at our deepest point of need and set us free. After a while the truth broke in upon this young man; we knelt and he wept his way to God.

"Dear God," he prayed, "forgive me for hating Dad all these years. Take away the hate." In a few minutes he jumped to his feet, smiling through his tears. I knew that God had touched his heart.

Then I pushed the phone toward him. "Here, call your dad. Ask him to forgive you."

He looked startled. "I can't do it! I haven't talked to my dad in fifteen years! He probably wouldn't even talk to me!"

"But things are different now," I encouraged. "You've asked God to forgive you for the hate. You've become a child of God. Ask God to help you."

He couldn't do it; finally he said, "Reverend Jones, I promise, I'll call him as soon as I get home."

As he left, I wondered what would happen.

Later he told me that when he called, his father was stunned to hear from his son after such a long time. "Dad," he said, "I'm sorry that I've hated you all these years. Please forgive me. I'm a Christian now; I love you. I want you to love me."

The father wept on the phone. He too asked forgiveness. Father and son were reconciled through Christ, and both gained the peace that had been missing for so many years.

Children learn values from the example of their parents. Our children learn to honor us by how they see us treating our parents. Do we gripe about "the old man" behind his back? Do we harbor grudges and ill feelings for past failings? Or do we work out the problems we have with forgiveness and grace? Do we treasure the presence of the elderly among us? Do we provide for their needs as they get older?

God loves to keep His promises. He desires to bless those who honor their parents from the heart. And families who honor their parents create a link of love and strength between the generations.

*6. "You shall not murder" (Ex. 20:13)*. Respect for human life begins in the family. Responding to pressures and problems with violence has become an alarming problem, even in the home. Wife abuse and child abuse are unthinkable crimes—but it's happening. And even when it's not happening in the homes, it's happening out in the streets. Young males think it's macho to carry guns; black on black crime is a serious issue in the cities.

Barbara Reynolds, *USA Today* inquiry editor writing in the newspaper's May 24, 1991 issue, comments: "We are witnessing the re-enactments in living color of the sordid acts that have been perpetrated on young people. Each day, many are being sexually, emotionally, and physically abused. They live on a daily diet of TV violence and hardcore, anti-human rap music, and they see people, sometimes their family members or neighbors, killed and maimed on city streets.

" 'Many youth, both urban and suburban, are suffering from post-traumatic stress,' says Jan Hutchinson, a pediatrician and a child psychiatrist. 'No one talks to them or intervenes to help. No one listens. We don't protect them. And they are angry. Their way of gaining control over their pain is to act it out on others.'

"Unless there are drastic changes, troubled youth can be counted on to continue acting out their worst nightmares," Barbara Reynolds continued. "As for the rest of us, we'll just have to remember to carry along our umbrellas."

Psychologists are saying that we are in danger of losing a generation of young black men, ages thirteen to twenty, if things continue to go in the direction they are now headed—if not to outright violence, then to drugs, or prison, or AIDS.

Unfortunately, most violence is between family members or people who know each other. We must begin at home, not only to instill a deep respect for human life, but to learn ways to deal with conflict in the home.

Jesus said, "You have heard that it was said . . . 'Do not murder. . . . ' But I tell you that anyone who is angry with his brother will be subject to judgment. Again, anyone who says to his brother, 'Raca,' [an expression of contempt] is answerable to the Sanhedrin [the court]. But anyone who says, 'You fool!' will be in danger of the fire of hell" (Matt. 5:21-22).

Why is anger and contempt a form of murder? Because it kills the human spirit. The young man we mentioned was on the verge of suicide because of his anger and hatred for his father. Verbal abuse of children can be as crippling and damaging as physical abuse—in some cases even more so. Some parents pride themselves that they never strike their children, but they dump anger and verbal abuse freely. Why are we surprised when that child grows up, gets a gun, and shoots someone in a fit of anger?

We must first of all ask God to give us as parents a deep respect for the fragile spirits of our children. Then we must teach our children that attitudes lead to actions.

Some parents allow their children to say, "I hate you!" And it's true that we shouldn't force our children to suppress their angry feelings; kids need to let off steam. But we can help them channel their angry feelings into nondestructive language as well as nondestructive behavior. Encourage an angry child, for example, to express himself and tell you what has made him angry, or if you already know, allow him to talk about how he feels without talking about hating you.

We must also help our children learn how to manage conflict. We will talk about this in more detail in a future chapter, but the home is a good laboratory; seemingly, kids are always fighting! Learning to identify the problem ("You scribbled on my picture and ruined it!"), ask forgiveness ("I'm sorry"), and *give forgiveness* ("I forgive you") can be valuable lessons that will help children deal with more serious conflict as they get older. Formally granting forgiveness is often overlooked; if someone says "I'm sorry," we might say, "Forget it" or "That's okay" — or just stay angry until the feelings blow over. But truly forgiving the other person can bring real freedom and reconciliation when a relationship has broken down.

There is one last issue that must be addressed in talking about respect for human life, and that is abortion. The issues that cause a young girl or woman to seek an abortion are complex; many are tragic situations. But the lives of millions of unborn have been snuffed out by this tragedy; many girls and women have been damaged spiritually, physically, and emotionally by aborting their children.

We must help our children understand that choices have consequences, and encourage them to ask God to help them make right choices. This is where strong values are critical: loving God, obeying parents, reserving sex for marriage, reverence for life. But what if a daughter becomes pregnant outside marriage? We encourage parents to forgive and counsel in love. The easy way out may seem to be abortion, but we believe God's Word clearly teaches that taking a life, though still in the womb, is wrong. The only possible exceptions relate to rape, incest, and saving a mother's life. We encourage parents to read what truly godly writers have to say on this subject, based on what the Bible teaches.

7. *"You shall not commit adultery" (Ex. 20:14)*. Teaching our children about sex is an important parental responsibility. Some parents feel uncomfortable or awkward and hope the school will do it. But our children are under a lot of sexual pressure from the media, from their peers, from changing social mores. If we don't deliberately teach sexuality from God's point of view, they will surely pick up their values somewhere else.

If phrased the other way around, this commandment would say, "You shall reserve sex only for the marriage relationship." This means that we must teach our children, first of all, that sex is a beautiful gift to be used only within the holy bonds of matrimony; outside of that it's sin. It's important to stress the goodness of sex, protecting it from attitudes and actions that would cheapen and abuse it.

Second, we must also teach that all other forms of sexual intimacy (fornication, adultery, homosexuality) are wrong. And therein is the problem. While society still generally frowns on adultery (breaking the marriage promise), modern social attitudes generally accept sexual intimacy outside of marriage between "consenting partners." But the Bible teaches that this is wrong (see 1 Cor. 6:9-20). Sex must be reserved solely for marriage. Wrong practice of sex has resulted in many of the heartbreaking social issues we face today: abortion, teenage parents, unwanted children, AIDS, other sexually transmitted diseases—not to mention a general breakdown in trust and commitment that impacts relationships when people do get married.

There is a lot of energy directed toward teaching "safe sex," especially after Magic Johnson revealed he was HIV positive—using contraceptives, especially condoms, to prevent pregnancy, AIDS, and other sexually transmitted diseases—but very little effort stresses the advantages and freedom of abstinence. Happily, later Magic did begin to advocate abstinence of sex outside marriage. At a recent youth night rally, I said, "In my judgment, safe sex is no sex apart from marriage." I was surprised when the crowd clapped and clapped and clapped. We need to help our young people understand that *God intends sex for marriage.*

Of course, there will still be people who will have sex outside of marriage. But that fact is very different than accepting that kind of behavior.

In order for our children to have the courage to say no to sexual pressure, we need to give them not only clear instruction, but the inner strength of a healthy self-esteem. When children feel loved and *valued,* they have less need to "follow the crowd" to gain acceptance and approval.

Richard Durfield, senior pastor of San Gabriel Valley Christian Center in Azusa, California, and his wife, Renee, developed a unique way to encourage their children to honor God's commandments regarding sex. As each child entered adolescence, the Durfields planned a special mom/daughter or father/son time (such as going out to dinner) for a "key talk." They talk covered many important issues, such as conception, the biblical view of marriage, and the sacredness of sexual purity. It was also a time to discuss the questions, fears, and anxieties of adolescence. Then the young person was presented with a "key" ring, symbolizing a commitment with God to keep himself or herself pure for a future marriage partner—a symbol of the key to one's heart and virginity.[3]

8. *"You shall not steal" (Ex. 20:15).* This commandment must be modeled within a context of being honest in all areas of life. If parents tell little white lies, fudge on their income tax returns, or make promises they don't keep, it's going to be hard for children to understand what's so wrong about snitching candy from a store.

A friend of ours realized the grocery clerk had forgotten

to charge her for a dozen eggs. So she went back to the grocery store to pay for the eggs. Her kids could hardly believe it. "Mom! It's not like it's your fault—it's their mistake! Why bother?"

"Because," she said, "if the clerk *overcharged* me for my groceries, I would certainly go get my money back. If I want the store to deal fairly with me, then I must deal fairly with the store."

We must also be honest with our children. If we borrow something, return it; if we make a promise, keep it; if we make a mistake, admit it and ask forgiveness. If we treat our children and their "stuff" with respect, they will learn to respect others and their things. We want our children to value integrity and trust between people more than getting money or things (though this often means respecting other people's money and things).

9. *"You shall not give false testimony against your neighbor" (Ex. 20:16).* How easy it is to gossip about people when they're not present—even our children! Children don't like their mistakes and foibles held up for aunts and uncles or neighbors to laugh about. Children want to know they can confide in you and you will honor their trust. This doesn't mean we can never get some counsel and advice about parenting from a trusted friend or counselor, but it does mean speaking of our children with respect, even when they're not present. And if your children hear you talking about others in a negative way behind their backs, they will fear that you will talk about them in that way too.

An even more dangerous kind of gossip is passing along hearsay information. "False testimony" rarely starts out as a bald-faced lie. Even a "true" statement, taken out of context, can give a false impression or create misunderstanding. And how often do we misrepresent the truth to protect our own skins? (It begins early in childhood when Tommy says, "Sammy did it!" Well, yes, Sammy broke the lamp, but only because Tommy tripped him!)

Too often we build ourselves up by tearing others down. This is common among teenagers who tend to indulge in a constant ritual of "put-downs"—which tend to mask their own insecurity. The easiest way to "look good" is to make someone else "look bad."

A good rule of thumb for a family is to never say anything when a person isn't present that you wouldn't also say if the person were there. Think about it! Would that change the way we speak about other people? About our children? About other family members?

What is true in the way we speak about individuals is also true when we're talking about groups of people. Just as we want to be judged on the basis of our character, not color, so we must do the same for others. Are we guilty of dismissing whole groups of people just because they're "rich folks"? "white folks"? "black folks"? "Northerners"? "Southerners"? "liberals"? "conservatives"? What attitudes about people are we passing along to our children?

It may sound simplistic, but as families we should look for good things to say about people—even ones who are difficult to like or get along with. This does not mean we should pretend real problems don't exist; it does mean developing a respect for others. It is a lack of respect for others that allows the weeds of prejudice, racism, bitterness, and violence to take root and grow.

*10. "You shall not covet... anything that belongs to your neighbor" (Ex. 20:17).* This commandment, like the two before, are different ways of stressing *honesty* and *integrity* in our dealings with people. It emphasizes our family priorities and what we value most. Is it relationships—or things? Do you feel competitive with others around you? If Uncle Clinton gets a new car, do you suddenly feel like you need one too? Are you always wanting more and more and never feeling satisfied? Are you working two jobs to "keep up with the Joneses"? Are you jealous of others?

This spirit of discontentment causes many families to

whip out the credit card and get themselves hopelessly in debt. Debt is a major problem tearing many families apart; the money is spent and owed before the paycheck even arrives. Some families borrow from friends or relatives to ward off the creditors, further straining relationships.

Of course, "coveting" a neighbor's wife can lead to adultery; "coveting" someone's wealth can lead to stealing. But even if we do not act on our feelings, jealousy and envy build barriers between people, and sometimes destroy the relationship.

We do our children and ourselves a favor if we cultivate a spirit of contentment in the family. The Apostle Paul wrote, "I have learned the secret of being content in any and every situation, whether well fed or hungry, whether living in plenty or in want" (Phil. 4:12). Avoid comparisons with others; learn to enjoy family activities that don't cost a lot of money; put relationships over material things; respect the sanctity of marriage (not only your own, but your neighbor's!); learn to budget your income.

If your children complain that other kids have a lot more money for clothes or bikes or video games, you may want to sit down as a family and show where the money goes. If you give a percentage of your money to the church or other charitable organizations, explain why that is important—even if it means less spending money.

Jesus warned, "Watch out! Be on your guard against all kinds of greed; a man's life does not consist in the abundance of his possessions" (Luke 12:15). He also promised, "I am come that [you] might have life, and that [you] might have it more abundantly" (John 10:10, KJV). God wants us to experience an abundant family life—but that abundance must come from the right sources.

### A Summary of Values

Have you noticed? All ten of these commandments were summed up by Jesus in this way: " 'Love the Lord your

God with all your heart and with all your soul and with all your mind.' This is the first and greatest commandment. And the second is like it: 'Love your neighbor as yourself.' All the Law and the Prophets hang on these two commandments" (Matt. 22:37-40).

The first four commandments speak to the importance of loving God with our whole hearts. The next six commandments show us how to love our neighbors (family, friends, strangers, enemies). Love God . . . love neighbor — these are the greatest values we can instill in our children.

But let's face it: these values are tough, easy to say and hard to do. A wounded child — abandoned by a parent, ignored or ridiculed, battered or neglected, craving attention or affection that's missing at home, or lacking positive role models — is going to find it hard to trust God, much less love Him. Such a child is going to feel angry, suspicious, and self-protective toward others, not love or respect for them.

Notice that Jesus said, "Love your neighbor *as yourself.*" Loving our neighbor grows out of a healthy self-love, a sense of security and love which enables us to reach beyond ourselves to others. This is where the fine art of parenting comes in (see the next chapter).

**Some things to think about and do:**
1. Talk together as a family about which of the spiritual principles (the Ten Commandments) discussed in this chapter are highly valued in your family. What events, interactions, attitudes, or behaviors among family members show that these are highly valued?
2. Which of the ten spiritual principles have not been given enough attention in your family? What difference would it make in your family if your family made a change in those areas?
3. What other values do you think are important to teach your children? Be specific.

## - 8 -
## The Fine Art of Parenting

*Keep yo' han' on-a de plow! Hold on!*
*Oh, Mothers, Hold on! Oh, Fathers, Hold on!*
*Keep yo' han' on-a de plow, Hold on!*
***Traditional***

**King David wrote,** "Children are an heritage of the Lord; and the fruit of the womb is His reward" (Ps. 127:3, kjv). An old Ashanti proverb states a similar thought: "Children are the reward of life."[1]

Is this how we view our children? All too often the modern parent seems to lose sight of this perspective. Children are an "unplanned pregnancy" that throws us into crisis . . . or around whom we juggle work, day-care, church, and community involvements.

We have justified this low priority on parenting with the cliché, "It's the quality of time spent with kids, not the quantity that matters." But Dr. Armand Nicholi of Harvard Medical School says:

Time and emotional accessibility are like the oxygen

we breathe. Although the quality of the oxygen is important, the quantity determines whether we live or die. A parent's inaccessibility either physically, emotionally, or both, can exert a profound influence on the child's emotional health. . . . What has been shown over and over again to contribute most to the emotional development of the child is a close, warm, sustained, and continuous relationship with *both* parents.[2]

Dr. Nicholi notes five trends which have made parental accessibility difficult today: (1) quick and easy divorce, (2) the increasing number of women in the work force who have young children, (3) the notion that to settle for the role of parent is "unfulfilling," (4) moving frequently or commuting long distances to work, and (5) the intrusion of television into family time. Dr. Nicholi believes these trends are "an extremely negative influence on family life—primarily because they contribute to a change in child rearing that has been taking place in this country during the past few decades. The change is this: in American homes today child care has shifted from parents to other agencies."[3]

The fine art of parenting begins with a commitment to *be* a parent. If we believe that children are a gift and raising them is important, we will give them priority time. This is true not only of the mother but the father as well. Let's look at what children need from their parents.

### Fathering

In times past, many fathers felt they had accomplished their parental duty if they kept a roof over the family's head, food on the table, and dispensed needed discipline from time to time. Unfortunately, even this basic fatherly role has degenerated. As previously noted, too many young men "prove" their manhood by getting a girl pregnant, but take no responsibility for supporting or caring for the child. And as discussed earlier, father absence or inaccessibility is a major factor in our family crisis today.

What, then, is the role of the father? Fathers must first of all reclaim the importance of providing financially for their wives and children, to be the buffer between the family and the pressures of society. To bring children into the world is to take on the responsibility for their well-being and safety. It is grossly unfair to leave our women to shoulder this burden alone. A real man will do all in his power to provide for his wife and children.

However, it is possible for fathers to do this and remain emotionally distant from their children. I would say even to fathers who are unemployed or feel they can't adequately support their families: *don't cut out.* The psalmist wrote: "I have never seen the righteous forsaken or their children begging bread" (Ps. 37:25). It may be not be easy, but God will make a way for those who trust Him. There are things even more important than money that you can give your children, which are essential to your children's well-being. The first and foremost is a *loving relationship.*

The involvement of a father in the lives of both his sons and his daughters is crucial to their emotional development and sexual identity. Christian fathers should take this role very seriously, for fathers are their children's first image — for better or worse — of what the Heavenly Father is like. Are you there when they need you? Do you listen to your children's thoughts and feelings? Do they feel secure and safe when they are with you? If they do wrong, is correction balanced with love and forgiveness, or are you too stern and inflexible? Are you often angry and unapproachable? Are your children afraid of you?

For sons, a father is the sex role model of what it means to become a man. A father helps a son differentiate himself from his mother and develop a healthy male identity. This is something that a mother can't do for her sons. If a father is absent, it's important for other men, such as a caring uncle or an involved grandfather, to help fill this role.

A father is also essential to his daughter's sexual identity. As a girl begins to see herself as a separate person from her mother, she looks to her father to affirm her feminine development.

"A woman's father is the forerunner of all other men who will enter her life and, consequently, he becomes her blueprint for the entire male species," writes Laura Randolph in *Ebony* magazine. "Because a father provides his daughter's first image of adult masculinity, he prescribes for all time her understanding of what it means to be a man."[4]

When the father relationship is absent, it can create serious problems for young women learning to relate in a healthy way with men. In fact, many girls who grow up without a father are often so hungry for a man—any man—to love them that they are very vulnerable to the pressures of men wanting sexual favors.

Once I was speaking to a large audience at a youth convention. I gave the invitation and a number of young people came to the front to receive Christ. The next afternoon my son, David, and I were sitting on the porch of our guest cottage when a young woman approached us and said, "I just wanted to tell you that what you said about the family last night made me very angry."

"I take it you did not come forward to receive Christ," I said.

She dismissed my comment with a laugh. "When I was about six years old, my mother brought me to this conference, and I went forward with her. But now that I'm in business for myself and have everything I want, I don't need God."

"What kind of business is that?" I inquired.

"I'm a prostitute," she said, and waited to see if I was shocked.

But I just asked, "How old are you?"

"Nineteen," she said.

I kept probing gently. "How did you get started?"

She sat down and told us a long story. She came from a very wealthy family, whose parents gave her and her four older sisters everything. Everything, that is, except love. "You see, my parents don't love each other. They're always arguing and fighting. One day after a bitter quarrel, I decided to take a walk. I had turned the corner when I heard a car pull up beside me—a beautiful white sports car. The driver called out, 'Hey, Baby. Let me take you for a ride.' I was frightened, so I shook my head and ran down the street. The car took off.

"About two weeks later my folks had another terrible fight, and I took another walk just to get away from them. Strangely enough, this same guy drove down the street and stopped. 'Hey, Baby, remember me?' he said. 'Get in the car and let's get acquainted.' That day I was so depressed because of my family situation, that I got in the car and went with him. We started dating and he said he loved me. But he was a pimp; he got me started in this business. Now he takes care of me. I've got everything I want—my own apartment, clothes, jewelry, expensive perfume, a car." She tossed her head proudly. "I'm not one of those prostitutes that walks the streets, you know. My clientele are up-and-up—doctors and lawyers—even some ministers come to see me."

"There's one thing you don't have," I said. "And that's peace in your heart. I know many nights after your client leaves and you're left alone, that you're miserable and empty." She was quiet a few moments and then nodded her head. So I went on, "That pimp doesn't love you. But God loves you. He can be your Heavenly Father to love and embrace you and care for you where your earthly parents have failed you."

I gave her my card and told her to call or write me if she'd like. About three or four months later I got a letter from her. "I'm writing to tell you that I gave my heart to Christ, and I found that peace you talked about." Starting over wasn't easy because her past life haunted her and she was afraid her pimp would find her and kill her. The last I heard, however, she was coming along quite well. But my heart ached for all the pain she had experienced because she didn't get that father love she needed so desperately as a young girl.

Dr. Kyle Pruett, author of *The Nurturing Father,* says, "Most children who end up without a father feel in some ways unfinished. A lot of children never develop a strong identity. As researchers, we know that boys never finish turning into men when their fathers aren't around, and girls don't finish turning into women. The deficit is really a big one."[5]

The good news, says Pruett, is that when fathers get involved with their children at a young age, caring for them, getting to know them, enjoying them, it's good not only for the children, but for the man as well. "A father who becomes an active part of his child's life knows so much more about the complexities of relationship. He's more patient. Nurturing fathers are described as more interesting people. . . . [They] lead more fulfilled lives emotionally and socially . . . [and] the children of these nurturing fathers are more resilient and tend to have a broader range of problem-solving skills."[6]

As our children were growing up, I was gone two or more weeks at a time for evangelistic crusades and other meetings. This was very difficult for me and my family. However, it was important that Wanda was there for them during these times, and she held the family together admirably during my absence and was always supportive of my ministry. But it is only in recent years that I've realized the impact these absences had on our five children. But the Lord helped bridge these stresses in our family life, and I always felt that it was a privilege to be a father. And now it's a joy for me to see our children grown, educated, married, serving the Lord and enjoying their families. I also find that being a grandfather is a very rewarding experience.

## Mothering

In many ways the role of mother is better understood because of the bonding that occurs between mother and child through pregnancy, birth, and infant care. But even this role is getting lost in the avalanche of modern social pressures for women to find a "fulfilling career" outside the home, even in the early years of their child's life.

Dr. Nicholi notes that "many young women no longer feel free to stay home with young children. Unless they pursue a career *while* raising the family, they consider their lives a failure. [But] my clinical experience indicates clearly that no woman with young children can do both *at the same time* without sacrificing one or the other, the quality of work, or the quality of child care. Many professionals *know* this—but few have the courage to say it."[7]

A woman should never have to defend being a mother at home, giving priority to raising her children. Wanda puts it in these terms:

As Howard's marriage partner, I see it as an awesome responsibility—a God-given opportunity to be the best woman, the best mother, the best wife, and the best grandmother that I can possibly be. But it's not an easy role to fulfill. In our situation, I have had many varied responsibilities. My husband was a pastor, then an overseas missionary, then an evangelist. It was a challenge to support him and be a loving wife, as well as sharing his ministry in many instances. As the children came along— one, two, three, four, five!—I felt responsible to bring them up in the fear of the Lord.

There are some preachers who say a woman's place is always in the home. This is too simplistic. There are many women these days who have to work—sometimes two jobs—in order to survive, especially if there is no male in the home. Women shouldn't be censured simply because they are working; the whole situation must be taken into consideration. And a woman has many stages in her life;

she may have many years before or after child rearing in which to use her talents and education in a variety of ways.

When we returned from Africa, I was asked to teach mentally retarded children at a nearby school. Even though my degree was in Christian education, not special education, I agreed to do it "for a while" — and ended up teaching for twelve years! Raising five children and working with people in a different culture in Liberia had given me some important skills and experience, even without a degree. I had found joy in staying home and being a mother, but I also found God gave me the strength and joy for this new challenge; it too was a rewarding experience when the timing was right.

However, I am concerned that women who marry give highest priority to their role of wives and mothers. It is a noble calling, and women have unique gifts for nurturing children and building the family relationship.

While fathers tend to hold their infants and young children away from their bodies and play with them, women hold their infants close. This body contact is essential for establishing a child's emotional sense of well-being in the early months and years.

Because mom is usually the caretaker, especially in the early years, children find comfort simply in her presence. If mom is absent from the home, for whatever reason, there is a void that can't be filled until she comes home again. I knew when I would come home from school, the first person I would look for was my mother. I would join her in the kitchen, munch cookies and milk, and talk about my day. When she died (I was twelve), coming home to an empty house after school was excruciating.

Women tend to be more sensitive to relationships than men. If a child is hurting, the mother will sense this. If something isn't working well in the home, the mother will often notice first and bring it to the attention of her husband. She is usually eager to get problems smoothed out and often plays the role of conciliator.

Mom is usually a child's first teacher and plays a tremendous role in character development: helping a child persevere in a task, share possessions, be honest, be kind. If men are taking seriously their role as provider, it often falls to the moms to train the children to do chores and keep up with their homework. Training and teaching, of course, is a task for *both* mother and father. It's especially important to agree together on how to train the children, or they will pit mom against dad and create disaster! However, it's often mom who has to carry out the battle plan, so it's vital for dad to back her up and give her support. (Children have an uncanny knack for discovering our weak points and wearing us down!)

A mother's example also sets the moral and spiritual tone for the household. It made a big impression on me to go past my mother's bedroom and see her reading her Bible or on her knees in prayer. When things got tough, her calm faith seemed to pull us together. She always taught us to never forget the poor, because "you may be in that situation some day," she'd say. During the Depression, many people would drift through our neighborhood and come to the door asking for food. My mother never turned anyone away.

I join Wanda in pointing out that one of the greatest gifts a mother can give her children is encouragement. Though limited in education, Mom Jones was always learning. She and my father were very knowledgeable of the history of black America, and told Clarence and me stories of black achievements. Our parents showed us the importance of setting goals and accomplishing them.

For Mother it was becoming a beautician. She and a close friend took a courageous step back in the '30s and enrolled as the first black American women students in an outstanding white school of cosmetology in Cleveland. The other students resented and rejected them because of their race. However, Mother and her friend withstood the pressures for two years, graduated with honors, and later owned and operated a successful beauty salon for many years in the city.

After my conversion, the Lord called me to the ministry. I struggled with the divine summons because I didn't want to be called a "Jack-leg Preacher"—someone who preached one thing and did another. But my mother would pray for me and say, "Howard, don't worry; God will make you a good minister." This helped me better understand and respond to God's leading in my life.

Mothers should be especially sensitive to the knocks and bumps of childhood as children venture out into the world. When a child comes to a mother for reassurance, how she responds will, first of all, affect her own sense of confidence in who she is, and second, will teach her how to deal with the problems she faces and the people she meets. For African-American families, this not only includes all the normal problems of growing up, but the painful reality of racial prejudice, which continues to increase, not only in society, but also in many churches.

When our David was in kindergarten, he came home from school one day crying. "Mother, what's the matter with my color?" he wailed.

"There's nothing wrong with your color," Wanda said, though her heart sank.

"Well," he sniffled, "some of the children told me I was the wrong color."

Wanda was tempted to get angry, march over to the school, and give the teacher a piece of her mind. However, she saw it as an opportunity to sit down with David and explain how God made everything in the world in a special way—including him.

"God made all the flowers with different colors and He also made people of various races, cultures, and nationalities throughout the world," she told him. "Some are black, some are white, some are brown, some are yellow, and some are red people as we see in America. God made you like you are; with God that's good. So don't ever let anybody make you feel uncomfortable because of your color or of who or what you are." David seemed satisfied and soon hopped off her lap to play.

But a child's self-esteem is fragile. We have pointed out that the presence of both mother and father in the home is an important ingredient in providing emotional well-being. But nurturing the self-esteem of our children so they grow up into confident, well-adjusted adults is an on-going task for single parents as well as two-parent families. Let's look closely at this challenge in the art of parenting.

## Single Parenting

Even though we have been emphatic about the important role fathers play in their children's lives, at the same time we want to encourage those single mothers who are going it alone. All is not lost. They have a tough row to hoe, but there are things they can do to strengthen and build up their families even without a mate. God is their source of strength; He has promised to be "a father to the fatherless, a defender of widows [women without mates]" (Ps. 68:5).

Some single mothers, especially in the black community, feel they have three strikes against them: being black, being a woman, and being a single mother. Welfare seems the only option—and in some cases it is—and they fall victim to the myth that they have no future. But single mother Sonya Henderson says, "For many young black women, especially teens who are mothers, welfare is the only means of survival. Women who choose to receive it should not be subjected to mockery. They should, however, understand its function. Welfare is public assistance to the underadvantaged. It is an aid to one's life, but it should never become a way of life."[8] Sonya Henderson tells how (after being abandoned by her child's father and a near-fatal suicide attempt) she realized she could let her situation defeat her, or she could triumph over her situa-

**117**

tion. She took advantage of the welfare benefits available to her to go to school, get on her feet, and become a full-time employee, as well as a dedicated mother.

But how can a single mother find the time, much less the energy, for the art of parenting? First of all, find prayer support with Christian friends. It's tough going it alone; it helps to share burdens with others who can help carry them to the throne of grace. Secondly, a single parent can find support for herself and her children through regular church participation. She should look for a church that has dedicated Christian men involved with the youth, either as Sunday School teachers or youth leaders. These "spiritual fathers" can help provide some of the role models and relationships with men her children need. Also, attending church together can give the single mother's family a sense of unity and strength that may be lacking if members go their own way.

What is the status of the child's father? If he is around and willing to be involved with his child, the single mother should encourage the relationship if at all possible. (Obviously, some men have abandoned their children, are abusive, or are abusing drugs or alcohol in a way that would be harmful.) The mother must not belittle the father in front of the children; they need to love and respect both parents. This, of course, is also true for fathers who are raising their children alone. The need of children to have a loving relationship with adults of both sexes is a compelling reason for a divorced or never-married parent to maintain contact with the noncustodial parent.[9]

Another relationship that should be cultivated is with the extended family. A child without a father in the home will benefit from regular contact with uncles and aunts, cousins, and grandparents. These extended family members can perform some of the developmental tasks that a parent alone is not able to do.

If a working parent (single or married) must use day care, he or she should choose carefully. Many churches run day-care centers; attention should be given to choose one that has a good reputation and a high ratio of caretakers to children. For instance, the Reba Place Day Nursery in Evanston, Illinois, a church-related center, has an open-door policy: parents are welcome to drop in at any time. This puts parents' fears to rest who have heard horror stories of child abuse in day care centers.

Last but not least, the single parent should not try to be "super parent" to compensate for the absent parent. It's not an admission of failure to ask for help. *All* parents, whether married or single, can grow in the fine art of parenting—especially in learning how to communicate with their children, and learning to discipline successfully. As we look at these next two areas in the next chapter, let's also resolve to pray for one another, support one another, and learn from one another—married and single parents alike.

### Some things to think about and do:

1. As a parent, what do you think is the most important thing *you* can give to your children? What changes might this mean in the choices you make day to day?
2. If you are a single parent, what types of support do you have in helping to parent your child, especially in providing relationship with a caring adult of the opposite sex? What types of support would be helpful to develop?
3. Read a book on parenting with your spouse (or another parent) and discuss each chapter.

**- 9 -**
**Train**
**Up a**
**Child**

*Footprints of Jesus, leading the way,*
*Footprints of Jesus, by night and by day;*
*Sure if I follow, life will be sweet!*
*Saved by the prints of His wounded feet.*
L u c i e  E .  C a m p b e l l

**While traveling by plane** to an evangelistic crusade, I noticed a mother and father with two small children seated nearby. As we were taxiing down the runway, the stewardess said to the father, "I'm sorry, sir, but you'll have to hold your daughter in your lap. She's too little to sit with the seatbelt."

"Well, I don't know—I'll have to ask my daughter," he said. "Do you want to sit on my lap, Honey?"

The stewardess said, "I don't care what your daughter wants. She has to sit on your lap; that's the law."

I was astonished when the father again said to the child, "Well, Honey, what do you want to do?"

At that, the stewardess got angry, and I didn't blame her. But to show her independence, the little tyke went to her mother and sat on her lap!

Another time Wanda and I were visiting a home where the mother asked her small son to do something and he said, "No."

"Johnny . . . " she pleaded.

"No, I won't!" he said defiantly and ran off.

The mother was embarrassed. She turned to us apologetically and said, "We can't do a thing with Johnny."

I thought to myself, "I'd like to have Johnny for about twenty minutes."

There is a great deal of confusion about discipline of children today. Parents are frightened by all the terrible reports about child abuse. So they hesitate to cross their children or impose limits. As a result, we see teenage "Johnnies" giving orders to their parents. Even in many Christian families, the kids are running the home. Some teachers refuse to teach junior or senior high school because the kids are so unruly, even threatening the teachers with violence.

These are conditions under which everyone realizes that something has gone wrong with the way a child has been raised. But where did it go wrong? Training up a child in the way he or she should go involves more than just "lowering the boom." Let's look at some of the fundamentals, which include—but are not limited to—correction for misbehavior.

### Building Self-Esteem in Your Child

In the last chapter we mentioned how important parents are in building a child's self-esteem, but we did not explain why this is so important or break the process down into its essential components. One of the symptoms of a poor self-image is when we cannot stand to allow others to rise above the level we see ourselves. This is demonstrated in constantly intimidating others, always needing to be right, and not being able to graciously receive correction. Gordon MacDonald says, "Self-esteem is a very important thing because somewhere in the middle of all this confusion [of the teenage years] there needs to be a sanctuary of sanity to which one can return and find the world right side up. Self-esteem helps teens know who they are. Plus, they need to know that their parents love and accept them, no matter what."[1]

In their book, *Just Me and the Kids,* Patricia Brandt and Dave Jackson explain self-esteem as a three-legged stool. The three legs might be labeled: (1) sense of worth, (2) sense of adequacy, and (3) sense of identity. They go on to explain the three elements as follows:[2]

*1. Sense of worth.* A child's sense of worth rests on whether he or she feels loved and accepted. Whether single or married, moms and dads are the most significant people for communicating this ongoing love. This love and acceptance is communicated in a variety of ways, all of which are important: direct statemetns ("I love you," "You're special"); hugging and affection; special remembrances (these don't have to be expensive gifts); the provision of necessities; and even fair discipline which says, "I care about you."

*2. Sense of adequacy.* A child's sense of adequacy is the feeling of competence, causing him or her to feel, "I can do it!" If children experience constant putdowns ("Can't you ever do anything right?" "Why are you always so slow?"), their self-confidence sags and the "three-legged stool" falls over. Because children usually look to the same-sex parent as a role model, Dr. Dennis B. Guernsey, director of the Institute for Marriage and Family Ministries at Fuller Theological Seminary, thinks it is the same-sex parent who contributes most to this sense of adequacy. That is, the father who has the most responsibility for instilling self-confidence in his son, and the mother is most successful in communicating the same to her daughter.

*3. Sense of identity.* A child's identity has two important parts: *a sense of belonging* and *a sense of being a unique person.* That is, a sense of belonging to the family group, and yet a sense of being a distinct member within it. A sense of belonging is created by family togetherness—developing family traditions, playing together, doing chores together, telling family jokes and stories, discovering your family tree, attending family reunions.

A child's uniqueness, on the other hand, can be celebrated by encouraging a child to develop his or her own special talents or hobbies, and appreciating what a child contributes to the family. Unfortunately, this aspect of self-esteem can be damaged if a parent constantly compares one child to another ("Why can't you be more like your brother?").

The identity leg of the self-esteem stool also includes a child's *sexual identity.* Both the mother and father are important in helping establish a child's healthy sexual identity. The same-sex parent, for instance, provides the role model of what it means to become a woman or man. But it is the parent of the opposite sex who affirms the progress that is being made along the way. A boy, for instance, may feel he'll never measure up to his strong, competent dad, but as Mom depends on him to do things which require his growing strength, he realizes he's becoming a man. His sexual identity is affirmed. In a similar way, a father can affirm that his daughter is delightfully different from him—even in the simple affectionate greetings, "How's my sweetheart?" and "Your hair looks great, Honey!"

Building healthy self-esteem in our children is not automatic, even in two-parent families. We need to understand the crucial role both parents play in either affirming and building up our children . . . or belittling them and putting them down. And even though a single parent can't be both mother and father to one's child, there are ways a single parent can compensate. One of these ways is to be deliberate about providing relationships for the children with role models of the same sex as the missing parent.

## Developing Good Communication

Another important parenting skill is good communication, both between the parents and with the children. Love and good intentions aren't always enough if family members misunderstand each other or miss what's really going on. Unfortunately, many parents don't come by this skill naturally. And when we finally figure out how to communicate with our preschoolers, suddenly they're school children and then teenagers; at each stage we have to start all over again!

We want to emphasize this point, not because Wanda and I have been perfect parents in this area, but because we're still learning and realize its importance.

Josh McDowell has declared, "You can have all the rules you want in a family, but if you don't have relationships with your children you are going to have rebellion instead of response. Good relationships are built on mutual respect. . . . Respect begins with listening. If you feel that someone is listening to you, you feel respected."[3]

Consider the following ways to develop good communication:

● *Concentrate on listening.* Strangely enough, the foundation of good communication is *not* talking but rather listening. One teenager said, "I try to share something with my parents, and as soon as I open my mouth, they start quoting the Bible. I don't want the Bible quoted; I just want them to listen to me."[4] It's so tempting to give our children "the right answers" before we've really heard what they're saying. Our daughter Lisa reminds us that when she was ten or eleven, she once came home from school upset because some of the kids had teased her with racial slurs. We tried to encourage her by telling her that even Jesus was persecuted. But what she really wanted was for us to just listen to her feelings. And it's true; even Scripture warns us, "Be quick to listen, slow to speak" (James 1:19).

Listening means more than saying, "Uh-huh," as our kids jabber away. We need to give them our undivided attention, put down what we're doing, and look them in the eye. We can ask a question to be sure we really understand or draw out our child, but we must fight the temptation to do all the talking ourselves.

*Find time to talk.* Concentrated listening often means finding time when kids feel free to talk. This doesn't often happen in the hustle-bustle of the day. Just before bedtime, when there are no distractions of phone, TV, homework, or visiting friends can be a good time to check in about the day's happenings. (It's surprising how many kids are willing to talk if it means delaying "lights out"!) Some parents schedule one-on-one time with each of their kids by going out for breakfast, taking a child along in the car while doing an errand, or going for a walk. A brief period of "debriefing" right when a child gets home from school, or when everyone gets home in the evening, is also a useful daily communication.

● *Learn your child's language.* In order to know what our children are saying when they talk to us, we need to "speak their language." If your child comes home banging doors and snapping at his or her siblings, do you react to the behavior—or ask yourself, "What's Mary/Johnny really trying to say?" Also, if we want to communicate with our child on his or her level, or even know how to ask intelligent questions, we need to understand something of our child's world. Do we know our children's friends? Their favorite music? The current fads and lingo? Do we care enough to be conversant about what interests *them?*

● *Be specific when you give instructions.* Don't expect your son or daughter (or your spouse!) to read your mind. It may be obvious to you that "come home early" means 10 o'clock, but unless you've been specific, your child may think "early" means by midnight. Don't just say, "Clean the living room" if you really mean vacuum the rug, straighten the newspapers, and dust all the furniture. The more specific we are when we give instructions to our children, the less misunderstanding and frustration there'll be.

● *Be willing to admit when you're wrong.* Parents aren't perfect. We know that; but here's the catch: our kids know it too! However, if we can't admit when we've made a mistake, our kids will feel it's useless to talk to us. ("Why talk to Dad? He'll never admit he was wrong.") However, if we're willing to say "I'm sorry," it paves the way for our kids to admit when they've blown it. Contrary to a popular misconception, kids don't lose respect for parents who admit when they're wrong. Rather, they learn to trust that we're real people, who will understand and accept them when they make mistakes, as well.

● *Keep your children's confidences.* Kids who risk sharing their deepest thoughts and feelings with a parent won't risk it again if the parent blabs to other family members, friends, or relatives. Respecting your children (and keeping the door to communication open) means respecting your children's confidences.

● *Take their thoughts, ideas, and feelings seriously.* It's so easy to brush off a child's opinion as irrelevant, or take a problem lightly. "Oh, you'll get over it," we say to some childish disappointment, or "Who asked you?" if a child ventures an opinion. To encourage communication, parents should look for opportunities to ask questions: "What do you think?" "How did that make you feel?" "What are you going to do about it?" "When we do this, we are communicating that a child is important to us, and what he or she thinks, feels, and does is important too.

Parents also need to be alert to "communication killers." Here are a few of the most common ones:

● *Uncommunicated expectations.* A lot of misunderstanding is the result of "assuming" instead of "communicating." A wife may assume her husband will know that saying "I'm tired" means "I'd like help with supper"; we assume our child knows not to eat all the Halloween candy at one sitting. Not so. If we jump all over our spouse and children for things that haven't been clearly spelled out, we have fights instead of communication.

• *Poor timing.* Just when a child is dashing out the door to school is not the time to unload your frustration about bad grades. Or when a child is playing with friends is not the time to ask, "Tommy, did you wet the bed last night?" We will get a better response from our children if we look for the right time to deal with problems—usually in private and when there's time to really talk about it.

• *Put-downs and cheap shots.* Sometimes we "communicate" our frustrations with so-called humor at our child's expense ("Yeah, Tina's wearing our vacation on her teeth"—referring to new braces). Or we hang labels on our kids, like "Clumsy" or "Stupid." The result is that kids tend to withdraw rather than risk being vulnerable.

• *Anger.* Unfortunately, if we yell at our kids or discipline them in anger, all our kids hear is, "Mom's mad!" and what we really want to communicate gets lost.

• *Always . . . never.* It's tempting to overstate problems: "Why are you *always* late?" "You *never* listen to me!" Kids will get defensive and the argument escalates . . . or else they'll back off and feel it's useless to talk to you.

• *Inconsistency.* If we say one thing and do another, it's going to go in one ear and out the other. Or if we tell them to do something and don't follow through, our children will learn they don't have to pay attention.

The art of communication is something we may have to work on all our lives. And it's never too late to learn communication skills to help improve our family relationships. Good communication also helps lay the groundwork in the area of discipline.

### Practicing Positive Disciplines

When children come to our Christian Family Outreach summer camps, they're confronted with the rules: "No radios or TVs . . . no smoking . . . get up when the bell rings . . . no foul language." Many kids rebel at these rules. "Nobody tells me what to do at home," they growl. But those that don't kick in, we send home. For those who stay, it's amazing what happens after two or three days, when they realize that we love them, and they can have a good time even with the rules. Then they simmer down, and some receive Jesus Christ as Savior. When the happy campers return home, their parents are impressed with positive changes they witness in their children.

If we are concerned about young people who are cutting short their lives through drug dealing and criminal activity, we must first regain control of our own children. Discipline begins in the home. But what is good discipline? How can a modern parent determine the difference between discipline and abuse?

The fine art of parenting means understanding the kinds of behaviors appropriate for children at different ages. As children explore, learn, and test the waters of their environment, there will be spilled milk, messes, and cries of frustration. But childish behavior is not the same as defiance. Little children are not miniature adults; we must allow for immaturity and accidents along the way.

At the same time, parents must take seriously the task of setting limits on behavior and guiding our children along the way. When we think of discipline, the first thing that comes to our mind is usually punishment. But discipline includes teaching, training, setting parameters, as well as correction for wrong-doing.

The Apostle Paul wrote, "Do not make light of the Lord's discipline, and do not lose heart when He rebukes you, because the Lord disciplines those He loves, and He punishes everyone He accepts as a son" (Heb. 12:5-6). Parents who truly love their children will discipline them, just as the Lord corrects us.

However, Paul also said, "Fathers, do not exasperate your children; instead, bring them up in the training and instruction of the Lord" (Eph. 6:4). The *King James Version* says, "Do not *provoke* your children to wrath [anger]." If our discipline is too harsh, we will create only angry, rebellious children.

We must avoid the two extremes: permissive parenting, which lacks control; and authoritarian parenting, which controls too harshly. It's important for parents to remember that *the goal of control is teaching our children self-control; the goal of discipline is teaching our children to be self-disciplined.* It's hard for us as parents to work ourselves out of the job! But that is our goal. If we set reasonable limits for our children, are consistent in our discipline, and couple firmness with love and affection, our children will grow in their ability to make responsible decisions on their own.

"What about spanking?" you may be asking. Young children cannot understand reasons for not running into the street or touching the hot stove. However, a spank on the hand or three or four swats on the bottom may help them obey when safety is the issue. Dr. James Dobson of Focus on the Family advises parents to reserve spanking for deliberate disobedience—not childish actions such as spilling the milk or forgetting to shut the door.

Spanking, as a form of discipline (Prov. 13:24) is part of a *process,* which includes communication between parent and child, and a resolution which includes forgiveness and reconciliation. This should not be confused with hitting a child, which is usually a *reaction* on the part of the parent who lashes out in anger or frustration. Children should not be jerked, slapped, hit, or otherwise physically manhandled in an uncontrolled way. In an article in *Family Life Today* magazine, Neta Jackson says that spanking is appropriate only for younger children and should include these ingredients:[5]

● *Do not spank in anger.* Give yourself a cooling off period; talk with your spouse or a friend, and consider what is the most effective punishment for misbehavior.

● *Talk with your child about why you are giving a spanking.* "You disobeyed Mommy (or Daddy)" is the key message.

● *Tell your child what to expect.* Tell the child how many swats you are going to deliver ("I am going to give you five spanks"). This is to let your child know you are in control.

● *Don't remove clothing.* If the bottom is too well padded, spank on the upper leg. You don't want any sexual confusion.

● *Assure your child of your love and forgiveness.* After the spanking, hold your child while he or she cries. Then talk again ("Are you sorry you disobeyed Mommy?"). If your child is repentant, be sure to hug and say, "I forgive you!"

As children get older, however, there are other forms of discipline which can be very effective. Let's explore some of these:

● *Direct communication.* We don't mean lecturing *at;* we mean talking *with* the child. If this is the child's first infraction of the rule, you might want to sit down and discuss what went wrong. You might discover it was a case of miscommunication or misunderstanding. Or if there's a problem affecting everyone, call a family council and have the whole family talk and decide what to do. Children will appreciate your not jumping to conclusions, and helping to decide the solution.

● *Logical consequences.* This is simply, "Let the punishment fit the crime!" If Mary doesn't pick up her toys when told to, you might remove the toys and put them away for a few days. If teenager Tommy comes home an hour after curfew, he loses his privilege of going out for a week. If you get a note from a teacher that Susie is missing ten homework assignments, it would be logical to ground Susie until all the assignments have been completed and turned in. This method of correction can be highly effective, though it sometimes takes careful thought and monitoring.

● *Loss of privileges.* This form of punishment can be used as a "logical" consequence; or it might be used even when it has no direct relation to the misbehavior. However, it's important that the loss of privileges (which might be watching TV, going out with friends, using the telephone, getting allowances, using the car) be something that *matters* to the child.

● *Grandma's rule.* This is known as "work before play," or roughly translated: Use what the child wants to do as a motivator to do what you want him to do! Grandma's rule can be used in simple situations: "I will continue reading the story as soon as you quit talking"; or more complex situations: "You may get your driver's license when you bring up those grades to a C average." It works best when stated positively ("You can go out to play as soon as the dishes are done" rather than "No, you can't play until you do those dishes").

● *Positive rewards.* Sometimes positive rewards can help children correct negative behavior. One little girl was touchy and threw a tantrum when her big brother so much as looked at her. This same girl also wanted pierced earrings. Her parents got a roll of "tickets" and told their daughter that when she earned fifty tickets (one ticket a day for not fussing at her brother), she could get her ears pierced. It took sixty-five days, but her parents proudly told her, "You not only look grown up on the outside with your earrings, but you've grown up on the inside too!"

Effective discipline isn't easy; we've made our share of mistakes. But we do our children a favor if we correct them in love. "No discipline seems pleasant at the time, but painful. Later on, however, it produces a harvest of righteousness and peace for those who have been trained by it" (Heb. 12:11).

**Some things to think about and do:**

1. Think about your own self-esteem. Do you feel secure enough in who you are that you can build up your children? Think back over the past week and name one way each that you have told your child: "You're special," "You can do it," and "You belong."

2. What new things might you do to improve your child's sense of worth . . . sense of adequacy . . . sense of identity?

3. What areas of communication need work in your family?

4. Read through the Book of Proverbs with your spouse (or another parent). What wisdom for parenting do you find?

- 10 -
Building
Family
Unity

*Dear Savior, let Thy gracious peace*
*Our homes and families bless;*
*Let love akin to Thine increase,*
*That bonds of tenderness ne'er cease*
*Throughout life's weary stress.*
Lois Stanley

**Maintaining the strength** of the family is a challenging job, even when everything is going relatively well. But we also need to be prepared for the rocky times, or they can tear us apart. In this chapter we will look at ways we can build family unity—first through working and playing together as a family, and then by strengthening our commitment to the family in the tough times.

### Developing Family Activities

Earlier we looked at the crisis confronting the African-American family. In too many cases the home has lost its influence; more and more kids are being "raised" on the streets. But one reason so many kids spend their time in the streets is because it's bedlam at home.

If the home can be a happy, attractive place, it can offset a lot of the temptations that come to kids on the outside. Let's look at ways we can make being together as a family a high priority.

## Good Times at Home

When my brother Clarence and I were growing up, Dad would take us fishing, spin tops, play marbles, fly kites, play baseball. Our house was the "headquarters" for the neighborhood — Dad had baseball bats and gloves and other things to share with other kids. He could be strict; Clarence and I knew we had better toe the line. As a plasterer by trade, Dad worked hard to provide for this family. But he was also a pal; he loved his family, and proved it in so many ways.

Wanda and I enjoyed happy times with our children as they grew up. We had fantastic times at Thanksgiving and Christmas and celebrated birthdays in a big way. We'd have family picnics, attend a circus, go to amusement parks, play and listen to music, go ice skating and fishing, and engaged in other sports. We would always find some fun things to do. Frequently, we'd go shopping at the mall, and enjoy eating out together.

I recall the time when our three daughters were invited to sing one evening during the Billy Graham Crusade in Cleveland. They had approached me earlier in the day and said, "Dad, Mother cannot go shopping today, so would you please come along and help us select three dresses alike?"

"Yes," I said, knowing from previous experiences that shopping with my wife and daughters proved to be a long, tiring experience for me. However, I was happy on this particular occasion that my daughters wanted their dad to accompany them.

"Girls, may I kindly suggest, however, that before leaving our hotel room, let's pause for prayer and ask God to please make this shopping trip a quick one." They agreed and we prayed and in the first store we visited near the hotel, we found three beautiful dresses exactly alike, with the correct sizes. It was a miracle, and we rejoiced together that God had answered our prayer.

One slushy winter day I took David and Phyllis with me to the mall. But Phyllis forgot her galoshes, so I just picked her up and carried her across the parking lot—that is, until I slipped on a patch of ice and she ended up sitting in a big puddle. She stood up dripping with water. And we began laughing hysterically, along with David and other shoppers who watched the whole incident.

When we were in Liberia, it seemed that we had more time to spend together as a family. The compound for radio station ELWA was right on the ocean, so going down to the beach was an easy way to have fun together. The kids went to school only half days and came home for lunch; Wanda and I were also home after our morning recording sessions. We all looked forward to the afternoons and evenings for special times as a family.

One day our seven-year-old David said the boys were getting together for a kite contest. "Would you make me a kite, please, Dad?" I didn't have materials to make a kite, so I said I couldn't do it. David was crushed until Wanda came to plead his case. So I prayed and asked the Lord, "What material could I use?" The thought came to use a sheet. So Wanda sacrificed one of her sheets. I went to the carpenter's shop to cut some sticks to my measurements, and we got the kite rigged up with a tail. We then made a test flight, and it flew, though kind of wobbly. David was excited, but I decided to make some more adjustments, and then the kite was ready.

The next afternoon was the contest, and many of the fathers came out with their kids and kites along the beach. At the signal the kites were lifted in the wind. The sea breeze carried David's kite above the other kites and over a nearby village and out of sight, and we won the contest.

David was overwhelmed with joy, and he still remembers that eventful day in his young life.

Today, David is an ordained minister, has pastored two Christian and Missionary Alliance churches, and is now a music specialist for Christian Family Outreach Ministries in Cleveland. His wife, Cora, is a guidance counselor at Westwood Junior High School in nearby Elyria.

During our pastoral ministry in New York City, our family would often go to the beach or to one of the city parks together. Many of the families from our church would do likewise, with picnic basket in hand. Almost all cities have areas for recreation—community centers where families can play basketball or swim, parks, bicycle trails. But don't fall into the trap of just "sending" the kids out; go with them.

In New York many of the parents who couldn't get out to the parks would come out in the evening, sit on the stoop and visit with neighbors as they watched their children play in the street. The children really enjoyed this because their parents were showing them attention.

Admittedly, we all have our busy schedules, but we need to set aside one night a week as "Family Night." No meetings, no telephone calls, no TV—just time to do special activities with the kids. Or it could be Saturday or Sunday afternoon. The important thing is regular fun times together.

But spending time together doesn't have to be all fun and games. Unfortunately, one of the most important family times is slipping away in many families today: *mealtimes*. We know some homes where the kids have their own microwaves in their rooms, so they don't even have to come to the kitchen for a snack! But when a family is too busy to even eat together, family life starts falling apart.

We have always thought it important to eat meals together. Mealtime is where we find out about each other's activities during the day. It presents the opportunity to be an encouragement or to discuss some problem that may have arisen. Some families put on the tablecloth and candles, even when it's not a special occasion, just to give the message: "It's special to be all together."

Families would be surprised how much time they'd have to spend together if they would turn off the TV. Most families do not realize how much power the TV holds over the family. (When we go to visit some homes, someone is usually sitting there glued to the television while we're trying to talk. If we want to pray together, some will turn the TV down real low but won't turn it off!) Not only does television spew out a lot of violence and other garbage, but it has replaced many other activities that used to bring families together: playing games, music and singing, reading, talking, doing crafts, playing outdoors.

Some families have had the courage to get rid of the TV altogether. But most of us have had to accept that television is here to stay, so we must learn to control it. Setting limits on the amount of time the TV can be on, preselecting only good programs for the kids, turning it off completely some evenings, choosing certain programs such as "The Cosby Show" and other wholesome programs to watch all together as a family, and taking advantage of some of the nature or educational programs are some of the ways we can rule TV rather than the other way around.

Reading aloud as a family is a wonderful together activity. When our children were younger, Wanda especially read Bible stories and other children's books with them. And as they grew older we read many of the classics. Just recently our youngest daughter, Lisa, asked if we still had her old Bible story book. When she was five years of age, she practiced reading it for herself—she probably read it through five times.

Lisa and her husband, Michael Granderson, live in Washington, D.C. She is the administrative service production manager for Thompson Publishing Group and Michael is a computer programmer analyst for *USA Today*.

Going to the library together and everyone getting books can be a great monthly outing. Choosing books to read aloud after supper (enjoyed by all ages) might include C.S. Lewis' Narnia series, the Laura Ingalls Wilder series about life on the prairie, biographies about black Americans who have made important contributions, etc.

Music can bring families together. Years ago a good percentage of black families had a piano. Someone in each family could play and the family would sing together. This meant children were introduced to music at an early age. An aunt or uncle who played another instrument might come over on a certain night each week and there would be a good sing. These get-togethers helped our children develop their musical talents.

Music is important to kids. Just look at the amount of time they are glued to their radios! But parents need to be aware of what they are listening to, reading, and watching on TV. As their father I couldn't understand or appreciate some of the music, it was so different from the music I had learned to appreciate. So I would go in and listen to some of the cuts from an album; sometimes I'd have to say, "No, you can't listen to this; the lyrics are off-color." So we'd have to work through that. It wasn't always easy, but actually listening to and discussing the music was better than just saying no to everything or ignoring it altogether.

Today an increasing number of black parents are also concerned that black films produced in Hollywood project most of the negative side of black American life, and leave a bad and distorted impression on the minds of our black youth.

News reporter Jack Harris wrote a provocative article on the matter. Here are some of his views:

Black filmmakers are caught between a rock and a hard place when it comes to subject matter for their products.

What sells in the marketplace is violence, sex and

rough language. So marketing decisions call for violence, sex and rough language.

"Boyz N The Hood" has grossed over $10 million since its opening. And although the principal theme involves a black father saving his son from the world of gangs, the movie is violent, full of sex, and some of the roughest language in film history. . . .

What are black filmmakers to do? They know what sells. Do they have special responsibilities because of conditions in black communities around the country? Yes they do! Gang life is but a fraction of what is happening in the black community in this nation. . . .

Because there are so few black films, the preponderance of violence, sex and rough language sends a wrong message to the world about African Americans.

Agreed . . . finding more productive film subjects is difficult at best. But with the black community under siege, often by its own members, there is the need for black filmmakers to work harder.

Every black person in America must join the struggle for the betterment of black life—filmmakers included.[1]

In view of this, let me challenge our white evangelical filmmakers to produce some quality films that will project the good and wholesome things being done by black American families.

### Serving the Community as a Family

Another way families can build family unity is by serving together in the church and community. Our first experience was many years ago. Wanda and I had graduated from the Missionary Training Institute, Nyack, New York (known now as Nyack College), and after we were married, I pastored Bethany C&MA Church for six years. It was during that time that Wanda started our three oldest girls,

Cheryl, Gail, and Phyllis, singing together as a trio in three-part harmony.

They were about three, five, and seven years of age, and they loved to sing in Sunday School and church services. Occasionally, Wanda would sing a solo or a duet with me in the meeting, or I'd play a musical number on my saxophone before preaching. The congregation enjoyed it. This served as a good example to them of our family ministry in the church and community.

As the children grew older I would take them along with me when I went calling on other families. Our kids began to feel a heart for people and ministry since they were part of it.

At radio station ELWA in Liberia, we were all involved as a family doing radio broadcasts. Wanda and I had weekly programs. Our girls, along with other children, did a broadcast each Saturday morning, called the "Happy Half-Hour." Occasionally, David sang solos with the group. Lisa was about five years old and kept busy playing with her little friends on the mission compound.

On Sunday afternoons, one of the ELWA missionaries came to our home in an old dusty, open Landrover to take our three oldest daughters to a nearby Liberian village for a children's service. The girls sang songs and told Bible stories using the flannelgraph. The children enjoyed the meeting as did the adults. Our daughters returned home, rather tired and covered with red dust from the roads, but praised the Lord for their missionary service for Him.

The point is: look for ways to include your children in the things that you do, especially in the areas of ministry and service. Serve meals at your local homeless center . . . if your gift is hospitality, give each child a responsibility preparing for or entertaining the guests . . . encourage the children to earn money for a family mission project . . . include a single mom and her kids on some of your family outings. Serving together will develop important spiritual bonds for your family.

## Setting and Achieving Goals

An important part of work, play, and service as a family is learning how to set goals and work toward them. One of the most important aspects of this is the example you set for your children. Do they see you trying new things? If you look around there are lots of opportunities for adult education: learning a language, learning a new skill, taking a literature class. If you haven't finished your education, if you're on welfare and need new job skills, it's never too late to achieve something that will better your life. If our kids see us setting new goals for ourselves and working toward these goals, it will set an important example for them.

But it takes action. We have to work with our children to give them the experience of setting realistic goals, deciding what needs to be done to reach those goals, and then following through. Part of this is teaching them the simple skills they need to get on in life. For instance, my brother Clarence and I were taught how to iron our own shirts and do other household chores when we were young (and I taught our son, David, too).

Because of our busy schedule while living in Africa, we had household help. But Wanda taught our daughters how to cook and care for their own clothes. Cheryl and Phyllis learned how to bake cakes and cookies, and Gail began to specialize in cooking macaroni and cheese. Lisa was too young to cook, but she did a good job of tasting everything. Now when we go to the homes of our daughters for a meal and compliment them on their cooking, they say, "Well, Mom, you taught us how to cook!"

When it came to taking care of their clothes, the children had a lot to learn, because they didn't realize what was involved in keeping them clean and mended.

But we can't just tell our children, "Learn how to mend. Do your own laundry!" We have to break it down into small steps so they can master each one. One of the best ways to do this is to work together, especially when you're teaching a new skill. (Working together also builds family unity; it's much easier to do chores when everyone is doing chores. It can even be fun! Put on some lively music, work hard, then engage in some worthwhile hobby when the job is done!) Of course, eventually children need to be able to do the job themselves. They won't always have Mom or Dad around to take care of the loose ends.

My parents taught my brother Clarence and me neatness in dress. We always had an inspection before we left the house for church and other places, and many times I was marched back to the bathroom for further attention. My parents always looked nice. But today you see many parents and children who don't seem to care about their appearance or conduct at home and in public places.

Appearance is important, especially in the African-American community when you go out to look for a job. It's necessary that we let our children know what's going to be expected of them. Today, competition for jobs is keen. If we don't teach children the necessity of a good education or of taking care of themselves properly, they will not be prepared for getting a job. We told our children, "When you walk in, you want to have a good appearance; you want to be able to speak properly. First impressions count."

Teaching children how to set goals and master skills around the home is good preparation for setting realistic career goals. Unfortunately, many of our black kids want to be a pop star like Michael Jackson, or they want to be a famous athlete like Michael Jordan or Barry Sanders, and only a very small percentage of these kids are going to make it in professional sports. But that's all many kids think of. I heard about a young man who had played football with an outstanding college, but felt dejected because he didn't make the pros. He had no other career plans or aspirations. Now he's into drugs, and his family is distraught. The athletic model was the only thing for him.

We tell the kids in our summer camps that there are other things in life besides sports. It's important, therefore, to discuss the future with your children. We need to present a broad range of career options. What about Christian service? Or does Paul want to be a lawyer? What are the steps to becoming a lawyer? Explore this together. Does Jayne want to be a nurse? Allan, a doctor? Do any want to teach children? Go into business? Program computers? Be a musician? Be a journalist? Build houses? Fix cars? Children should get involved in activities in the school and community which give them experience in these areas. But they need our support as parents to encourage them.

Giving our children a realistic and hopeful outlook on their future can strengthen them when they face setbacks and disappointments.

## Commitment to Family in Tough Times

Every family faces tough times. I recall a very traumatic experience we encountered a year ago. My wife joined our team for a weekend of meetings. After speaking to a group of women, she became ill, with vomiting and some loss of vision in her right eye. We rushed Wanda to the hospital, where two doctors examined her and advised me to fly her back home immediately. Back at the motel, my team members—crusade director Dr. Walter Grist; his wife, Janeva; Steve Musto; and C. Edward Thomas—joined me in prayer. They agreed to continue with the meetings so that we could leave for home.

On the plane Wanda worried about her vision, and would at times say, "Howard, at times I can see you clearly, but then you completely drop out of sight." It was a real scary experience, but we'd hold hands and pray for strength and safety in travel. When we reached home in Oberlin, Wanda was admitted to the hospital.

Our doctor examined her and discovered that she had

suffered a stroke. He decided to send her to another hospital for further tests and treatment. Wanda and I were stunned by the news, but encouraged our hearts in the Lord and His Word. We knew that God always engineers our circumstances for His glory and our good, according to Romans 8:28.

I went home and called our children, other relatives, our pastor, and friends for their prayer support. The next day, I phoned the Billy Graham Team office and asked for prayer for my wife.

The following morning I received a call from the doctor at the Elyria Memorial Hospital. He said that Wanda had definitely suffered a stroke, and there was bleeding in the brain, and that surgery was needed immediately to save her life. I urged him to proceed with the operation.

Before leaving for the hospital, I paused for prayer to commit Wanda to God's care and to ask Him to work through the surgeon and his team. I then looked out the window and saw a large beautiful dove on the porch. The bird walked about slowly, paused, hopped down the steps, and flew away. I believed that God had sent the dove, a symbol of the Holy Spirit and peace, to quiet my heart and assure me that Wanda would be all right.

My daughter Gail and others joined me in prayer as Wanda was taken to surgery, which lasted almost four hours.

Two hours passed and my dear friend and colleague in the ministry, Billy Graham, called and expressed his concern about Wanda. We prayed together on the phone for her recovery.

The operation was a success. The doctor assured us that Wanda would be fine. Later in the recovery room she recognized everyone and we praised God for answered prayer. After ten days she came home. In the ensuing weeks, she made frequent visits to see the doctor. He was always impressed with her progress, and would say, "It's simply amazing—amazing." Yes, we knew that God had worked a miracle in answer to prayer.

During this time Wanda was encouraged by phone calls from Ruth Graham, Cliff Barrows, and other team members and friends across the country. We were informed that delegates at the General Council of the Christian and Missionary Alliance had paused to pray for Wanda's complete recovery and health.

Today Wanda is enjoying good health, her vision is normal, she drives the car, teaches at a women's Bible study meeting each week, and speaks at various meetings. Tough times do come to families. But when a family knows the Lord, prays and trusts the promises of God, they can be sure that God will always give comfort and strength to go through troubles and trials. The psalmist says: "God is our refuge and strength, an ever present help in trouble" (Ps. 46:1).

The sickness, death of a loved one, unemployment, debt, abuse of alcohol and drugs, fighting, and disagreements are just some of the difficulties that constitute "tough times" for families. How do we maintain family unity in the hard times?

### Beyond Divorce

Many people see only two options when the family is falling apart: divorce or staying in a miserable marriage. But the Rev. Willie Richardson, pastor of Christian Stronghold Baptist Church in Philadelphia, says there is a third option: "Change! Learn to love each other and work out your problems!"[2]

Evangelist Luis Palau says, "To protect your marriage, I encourage you to learn how to identify and overcome five typical underlying reasons for divorce." In brief these are:[3]

*1. Unreasonable expectations.* We tend to expect a husband or wife to fulfill all our needs, to be the perfect mate. "Sometimes the key to improving our marriages is bringing our expectations down to earth," says Palau. Rather than depreciating our mates for their imperfections, learning to appreciate their good qualities can radically change our way of relating.

*2. Ungodly focus.* The wrong focus can make us feel dissatisfied with or create tensions in the marriage. Some people focus on their children, others on themselves, some on their careers. The only true focus is Jesus Christ at the center of our marriages, which helps us keep a godly balance.

*3. Uncontrolled passions.* Too many marriages are wrecked because of unbridled appetites for material things resulting in uncontrolled spending, sexual pleasure sought outside of the marriage, or chemical crutches. But Scripture tells us to "flee the evil desires of youth" (2 Tim. 2:22). Self-control (a product of the Spirit—see Gal. 5:22) is essential for family unity.

*4. Unforgiving attitudes.* All of us have shortcomings. All of us fail. All of us need forgiveness. If we harbor unforgiveness toward our mates, it will strain and crack the marriage. But Scripture encourages us to "forgive as the Lord forgave you" (Col. 3:13).

*5. Unbiblical presuppositions.* Some people play games with the Word of God to justify their actions. But both the Old and New Testaments lift up marriage as a spiritual metaphor of our relationship with God. The emphasis is on faithfulness and sacrificial love. Jesus said, "What God has joined together, let man not separate" (Mark 10:9) and " 'I hate divorce,' says the Lord God of Israel" (Mal. 2:16).

When families face tough times, it's important for family members to renew their commitment to the marriage and to the family. Even major problems can be dealt with if both partners have the attitude, "With God's help, we're going to face these problems together."

Unfortunately, too many couples try to do this alone. They don't want others to know they're having struggles, or they feel hopeless that anything can be done. So they just gut it out, cover it up, or ignore what's happening until their marriage or family is a shambles.

The problems many black American families face today are real. We need all the help we can get. This book is one attempt to give men and women, fathers and mothers, a vision for the family and handles on the challenges they face. But a book can't solve anything; it can only help point you in the right direction, beginning with the Lord Himself.

In the back of this book there is a list of resources for the family, such as Recovery of Hope, a network of peer support groups and counseling centers to bring hope to hurting marriages. Your pastor may be able to give you needed counsel or direct you to people or organizations for help.

Above all, study the Bible, get on your knees and pray for your marriage, your spouse, and your children. God cares. He wants to make a way. But you must be prepared for Him to do a work within your heart, lifestyle, and habits.

### Problem-Solving and Conflict Resolution

All family members must learn how to deal with each other's differences. "Just because husbands are men and wives are women is grounds enough for disagreement," quipped one couple.[4] We may have differing expectations for marriage and family life, disagreements about raising children, different temperaments, different family experiences when we were children. Some of these differences enhance and enrich our relationships; other differences seem to cause conflict.

Conflict isn't bad in and of itself; it's a normal part of marriage and family life. Whether or not conflict strains family unity depends on how the conflicts are handled. And little problems can become big problems if family members do not know how to handle their conflicts in a healthy way.

Marriage counselor Norm Wright, in his book *The Pillars of Marriage,* suggests five ways husbands and wives (and parents and children) have of dealing with differences.[5]

1. *Withdrawal.* One or more family members think conflict is not worth the effort, especially if previous conflicts proved negative and didn't solve anything. Changing the subject, not talking, spending more time apart, avoiding topics of disagreement are all symptoms of withdrawal.

2. *Winning.* Winning or proving one's point becomes the major objective. One person must be right, and the other person wrong. This style of conflict often involves arguments, verbal fights, attacking the other person, making judgments. The response is usually counterattacks or becoming defensive.

3. *Yielding.* We must all yield sometimes, but yielding can be a means of protecting oneself. We just give in and let the other person "win" to avoid further unpleasantness. Anger tends to pile up, however, and eventually comes out.

4. *Compromise.* Though compromise sounds good, it is based on giving a little to get a little. It focuses primarily on the solution, and not the process (understanding feelings, different ways of thinking, past experiences). Unfortunately, one or both may feel some resentment over what was lost.

5. *Resolve.* Truly resolving a conflict starts with direct, loving communication. Each person tells his or her needs and feelings; each person listens to and tries to understand the other. There is no attacking or judgment of the other. Though yielding or compromise will sometimes result, the understanding sought in this approach ideally helps the parties come to mutual agreement on the resolution.

When families understand their own "style" of conflict, they can often make adjustments to reach a better outcome. Some other tips for "fighting fair" when dealing with a conflict: stick to the topic—don't bring up old problems; avoid name-calling and words like "always" and "never." If you're angry, take some time to cool off before trying to resolve the conflict; be willing to apologize if you "break the rules." When the argument is over, a hug can help smooth ruffled feelings. And it would be good to pray together.

Marriage seminar speakers Randy and Therese Cirner say, "The first and most important principle we've learned [to handle disagreements] is to practice preventive medicine. We've found that by setting aside a specific time each week—yes, each week—to talk about the details of our separate lives, we prevent a number of disagreements from ever happening. *Good communications is the best preventive medicine.*"[6]

Scripture is also helpful in understanding how to resolve conflict. Jesus said:

> If your brother sins against you, go and show him his fault, just between the two of you. If he listens to you, you have won your brother over. But if he will not listen, take one or two others along, so that "every matter may be established by one or two witnesses." If he refuses to listen to them, tell it to the church; and if he refuses to listen even to the church, treat him as you would a pagan or a tax collector (Matt. 18:15-17).

Jesus was speaking, of course, about settling disagreements between fellow believers. But there is truth here for married couples as well. First, if you have a grievance, go to your spouse alone. Talk about it together and do your best to work it out in private. But if you cannot work out the problem between you, then go together to talk to someone else who can give you spiritual and relational counsel—a pastor, an older Christian couple, or a marriage counselor. If the problem is serious or complex, it may mean extended marital counseling by a professional. Most matters should be able to be cared for in this two-step process.

If the problem cannot be resolved, a Christian may need spiritual counsel from his or her pastor or church elders. There are other Scriptures which help us understand how a believing wife should relate to her unbelieving husband, for instance, or how to respond if a spouse is adulterous or pursues a divorce.

### Forgiveness

We cannot stress too much the healing power of forgiveness. Our marriages and family situations aren't perfect; we *will* fail each other; we often hurt each other by our thoughtlessness or insensitivity. We will face tough times that strain our unity with one another. But God's gift of forgiveness is the key to unlocking the doors of bitterness and anger that may be destroying our families.

It has been said that "a good marriage is made up not of two good lovers, but of two good forgivers."[7] When we are willing to forgive, we thwart Satan who likes nothing better than to drive a wedge in our relationship with each other. When we feel hurt or unloved, Satan capitalizes on our natural human reactions of resentment, anger, and desire for revenge by building walls of bitterness between us. But God has a different method:

> Now instead, you ought to forgive and comfort [the one who has caused you grief], so that he will not be overwhelmed by excessive sorrow. I urge you, therefore, to reaffirm your love for him. . . . Forgive . . . in order that Satan might not outwit us. For we are not unaware of his schemes (2 Cor. 2:7-11).

Forgiveness is important, not only for the sake of others, but for our own benefit. For one thing, God's forgiveness of our own weaknesses and failings seems to be connected with our ability to forgive. Jesus said, "If you hold anything against anyone, forgive him, so that your Father in heaven may forgive your sins" (Mark 11:25). For our own spiritual health, we must seek to forgive and be forgiven.

Lewis Smedes, author of *Forgive and Forget,* adds that we do ourselves a favor when we forgive. "Suppose you never forgive, suppose you feel the hurt each time your memory lights on the people who did you wrong. And suppose you have a compulsion to think of them [or your hurt] constantly. *You have become a prisoner of your past pain.* . . . The only way to heal the pain that will not heal itself is to forgive the person who hurts you. Forgiving heals your memory as you change your memory's vision."[8]

Forgiveness changes the conditions under which our family relationships can grow and thrive. We don't have to be anxious that we'll make a mistake. (We are going to make mistakes; there's no avoiding that.) If we develop the freedom to ask for and give forgiveness, small things can remain small. We can pick ourselves up and go on . . . together. But even relationships seemingly broken beyond repair can be mended when one person is willing to say, "I'm sorry," and the other, "I forgive you."

**Some things to think about and do:**
1. What kinds of family activities might help strengthen your family unity? List two or three that you plan to implement in the next month.
2. Brainstorm possible ways you and your children can serve your church or community together. Choose one that makes use of each family member and go for it!
3. What is your "style" of handling conflict (withdrawal, winning, yielding, compromising, resolving)?. What changes do you need to make to resolve conflicts in a healthier way? Ask God to help you make those changes.
4. Are you holding anger or bitterness in your heart against your spouse, ex-spouse, or other family mem-

ber? Ask God to help you forgive him or her. Seek help from your pastor or another mature Christian to help you thwart Satan's plan to drive the wedge of unforgiveness between you and your spouse.

5. If you are already divorced, what have you learned from your experience to help you relate in a godly way to your ex-spouse? In a possible second marriage?

- 11 -
The
Black
Church
and the
Family

*We've come this far by faith*
*Leaning on the Lord;*
*Trusting in His Holy Word,*
*He's never failed me yet.*

A l b e r t   A .   G o o d s o n

**Doris was tough.** By sheer grit she had survived when her husband abandoned her and their little boy, Nate. She worked hard to support her child, and went to the bars at night to help fill the lonely places in her life. When Nate was ten, she got pregnant again—a sinful one-night fling with someone she met in the bar. She didn't want this child; how was she going to support another one? But stubborn and stoic, she struggled on. "My little girl turned out to be . . . how do you say it? . . . a blessing," says Doris now.

Doris' children wanted to go to Sunday School, so young Nate took his little sister to the Detroit Afro-American Mission. They begged Mommy to go, but she had no use for church. Doris was too sophisticated for that religion nonsense, she said. But the children didn't let up.

One day Robbie looked at her mom sadly and said, "Mommy, when you die you're going to hell."

Her daughter's words shocked Doris and she began thinking about it. Was there more to life than struggling to make ends meet and looking for the right man to end her loneliness? So one Sunday Doris went with her children to the mission.

The people at the mission acted as if she were an old friend! They hugged her and told her how glad they were to see her. "We want you to come back!" they said. "Your children are so special." Doris was dazed. All her life she'd struggled with feeling worthless and cast off, but these people made her feel wanted. One day while attending a special service with her children, Doris was asked by a kind sister if she would like to pray with her. In a little side room, Doris asked Jesus to be her Savior and the Lord of her life.

"All my life I'd had such a bad self-image of myself," says Doris. "But God came into my life and showed me that I am the temple of the Holy Spirit! I am unique, His special creation, and He loves me!"

Doris now sees Nate establishing a Christian home with his wife and two little girls, being the kind of father he never had. As for herself, Doris says she still struggles with the desire "to be with men," but she has learned that prayer and the support of her brothers and sisters in the church is very important to living as a single.[1]

In the midst of personal crisis, it is easy for the individual family to feel overwhelmed. And faced with the overwhelming statistics regarding the crisis in the black family in America today, all of us are tempted to feel despair.

But the Rev. Willie Richardson, pastor of Christian Stronghold Baptist Church in Philadelphia, is not discouraged. "I believe the family can turn around," he says. The key, Richardson believes, is the black church.[2]

In his book *The Church in the Life of the Black Family,*

Wallace Charles Smith points up the interconnectedness of the church and the family for African Americans:

> The black family's chief strength is its extended nature. . . . Two skills which have allowed for the survival of the black family throughout the period of slavery and beyond are its adaptability to change and its extended (rather than nuclear) structure. . . . The knowledge of these important family attributes is crucial to the task because the black church is an extension of the black family. . . .
>
> The black church in America developed out of the deprivation and oppression experienced by the slaves. In so doing, the black church existed as a support system for the oppressed at society's breakpoints. Without question the worst break point in this slavocracy was the separation of family members from one another. Mothers, fathers, sons, and daughters were consistently sold away at the masters' whims. The church evolved as a new family for those who were continually being uprooted from their original families.
>
> Sadly for many blacks, the secularization of the twentieth century has exacted a great price. The church no longer occupies the central position of authority in the life of blacks that it once did. This fact has a great impact on the family.[3]

Today we desperately need to witness a moral and spiritual awakening in black America, and this must start with the church. If African Americans are going to find the strength to rebuild their families, and the support needed to overcome the destructive pressures and problems of everyday living, it's going to be through a spiritually revived church, God working through the church for His glory and for the good of His people.

The spiritual revolution, then, is not going to come through a new political order; it's not going to come through blue-ribbon studies or government money or social organization. All these are helpful and needed, but fundamentally the frightening conditions and problems that plague us will not change until the hearts and lives of people are radically changed through a personal encounter with Jesus Christ, the crucified and risen Son of God, our living and loving Savior, and eternal hope. "Therefore if any man be in Christ, he is a new creature; old things are passed away; behold, all things are become new" (2 Cor. 5:17, KJV).

## The Importance of the Black Church

Many years ago, noted black scholar Dr. William E.B. DuBois, aware of the history, development, and importance of the black church of America, gave his evaluation of it in his classic book, *The Souls of Black Folk:*

> The Negro church . . . is the social center of the Negro life in the United States, and the most characteristic expression of African character. . . . At the same time this social, intellectual, and economic center is a religious center of great power. Depravity, sin, redemption, heaven, hell, and damnation are preached twice on Sunday with much fervor and revivals take place every year . . . and few indeed of the community have the hardihood to withstand conversion. Back of this formal religion, the church often stands as a conserver of morals, strengthener of the family life, and the final authority of what is good and right.[4]

Even today, the black church stands unchallenged as the oldest, most powerful, and most influential of all other black institutions. While there have been and are black congregations within white denominations, the most authentic "black churches" were founded and led by African Americans. The black church is a preserver of our spiritual heritage, history, and culture, and continues to champion the cause for civil rights and other issues necessary for the welfare and progress of black America.

Dr. Otis Moss, pastor of Olivet Institutional Baptist Church in Cleveland, Ohio, comments:

> The black church has been a solid rock for African Americans, in the face of the devastation of our social institutions. When our families were torn apart, our enterprises usurped, our national affiliations erased, and our possessions destroyed, the black church flourished to sustain African Americans throughout our ordeals.
>
> More importantly, the black church gave African Americans the means to develop the energies, strategies, and abilities to overcome these ordeals that we faced throughout American history. The black church gave African Americans the community, consistency, concern and competency to survive and at times even to thrive amid adversity. It was the only institution in the past and, for most African Americans, in the present, to be owned and operated solely by blacks. As such, it gave African Americans the only opportunity most of us have had to develop leadership skills as well as to nurture our self-confidence and self-esteem, even in the face of great adversity.[5]

Preston Robert Washington, pastor of Memorial Baptist Church in Harlem, New York, agrees but goes a step further. He says, "The church is the single most prominent and important institution in the black community. It is both terrifying and challenging to realize that as the church goes, so goes the community, the nation, and in large measure, the world . . . ; hence it has been given a sacred stewardship trust to become all it can be as an instrument of God's transforming Spirit."[6]

Today, however, the black church faces one of the greatest challenges of all times: the plight of black America and the crisis in the black family. The fact that not just black families but families throughout America are in crisis today is an indictment upon the church, white and black alike. There are many notable exceptions, evangelical churches that preach the Gospel in all its fullness to the hurting persons and families in their communities, and these churches continue to grow.

But we also witness many other churches—those like the church at Laodicea, spoken of in the Book of Revelation (3:14-22)—that are lukewarm in the love for God and people. These churches displease the Lord and lack the spiritual power to reach an increasingly sinful and skeptical society.

For better or worse, the black church has more power than any politician, because thousands and thousands gather every Sunday for worship. If we accept that premise, then the black church has a tremendous responsibility to the community. If the black church is going to meet this need and be a force in this crisis, we desperately need to see a renewed spirit within our churches.

## A Call for Renewal

While talking with a black businessman in New York a few years ago, I asked, "As you observe the black church today, what is your feeling about it?"

The man thought for a moment and replied, "Dr. Jones, I sincerely believe that the black church in America must experience a true revival of the Holy Spirit, because for the most part, the church is failing to provide a moral and spiritual dynamic we so desperately need to change our situations and enhance the quality of our life and families and communities."

This was an astute observation, one we believe is still true today. The black church must realize that the *greatest* need among black Americans today is neither freedom from the blight of racism and discrimination, nor the securing of civil rights, as great as these social, political, and economic needs of our people are. Underneath these realities is a more paramount one, a spiritual need. As a people we need to witness a moral and spiritual awakening, for we have drifted from God and from the moral and spiritual realities that are revealed in Jesus Christ and in the Word of God.

Why has the black church become spiritually impoverished? First, the church has lost the vision of the purpose of the church; and secondly, the church has drifted far from the divine pattern and program of the church. Let's consider what this means:

• *The church should be a place for divine worship.* We come together to worship *God.* Unfortunately, in too many churches, the focus seems to be on what *we* need. We've been in churches where Bibles are hard to find. Sunday morning worship in particular should be a time of corporate worship and praise to our Lord and Savior, Jesus Christ, along with exposition from the Word of God.

• *The church should be a place for Christian fellowship.* The church should be a family of the redeemed, people seeking to satisfy the requirements of membership in the family of God and heeding the call to be true disciples. Some churches are so anxious for members, they simply ask those who want to be a member of the church to come forward and receive the right hand of fellowship. Many of these folks may be sincere and well-meaning and may become good workers in the church, but some have never experienced conversion.

• *The church is to reflect the holiness of God.* While conducting revival meetings in Delaware, a local pastor invited me to go visiting in the neighborhood. As we approached one house, the pastor said, "Howard, the man here was once an alcoholic, but he was converted and became an outstanding Christian layman in our church. However, something went wrong in his life, and he slowly drifted from God and returned to his old sinful ways. We have tried many times to get him back to church, but he's not interested."

We entered the home, visited with the man a while, then I invited him to our special meetings. He declined. When I asked why, he said, "Because I don't believe in playing with God. You see, Preacher, I once knew the Lord. Christ delivered me from a life of drunkenness, and for a time I served God in the church. But after a while I got out of fellowship with God, and the devil led me back to my old ways. So I stopped going to church. But," he said, jabbing a finger toward us, "there are plenty of other people in the church who aren't living right either. On Sunday I see 'em going to church; they sing and shout, but I know for a fact that they live just like the rest of us the rest of the week. Occasionally I see some of the deacons duck into a nearby alley, take out their bottles and drink, then walk on into the service as though nothing had happened.

"Now, sir," the man concluded, "if your preaching helps those hypocrites get right with God, perhaps I too will come back to God and the church. But I don't see why I should sit with those who live just as I do, but try to give the impression that they're saints."

He was right to a point. Today church members must exhibit more than just an outward form of religion and emotion displayed in singing, shouting, and preaching. They need to manifest the holiness of God in their character and conduct.

● *The church should exercise spiritual discipline of its members.* The early church exercised the rule of discipline among its members. Ananias and Sapphira are the most notable examples. This couple plotted to lie about the nature of their offering to the church. The Holy Spirit revealed their sin, and swift judgment and death followed (see Acts 5:1-11). The Apostle Paul encouraged the Corinthians to discipline one of their members who was guilty of immorality, so as to maintain the purity of the church (1 Cor. 5:1-5). But the rule of discipline has almost vanished from modern church life. Leaders and members alike can sin and walk contrary to the Word of God without fear of discipline from the church. How can we have a healthy spiritual church, one possessed with the power of God, if there is no standard of righteousness, and church members are not disciplined when they do wrong?

• *The church is to be a place for prayer.* We must return to a ministry of prayer. Prayer is the Christian's mightiest weapon in our spiritual warfare against Satan and the world (Eph. 6:10-18). Jesus said, "Where two or three come together in My name, there am I with them" (Matt. 18:20). There is power in uniting our hearts and voices in prayer. Whatever weaknesses we may be experiencing in our churches, whatever crises affect our individual members of families, whatever challenges we face as a black community, prayer should be our first attitude and our first action.

But, regretfully, we have far too many prayerless churches. There may be tremendous crowds on Sunday mornings, such as Christmas, Easter, and Mother's Day. People will turn out for choir practice and social and political meetings in the church. But what about the attendance at the church prayer service? The weakest meeting in most of our churches is the prayer service. Many churches have had to discontinue the midweek prayer and Bible study meeting because the people have ceased to attend.

In prayer we acknowledge our need for God; in prayer we call upon the resources of heaven. Robert Washington, pastor of Memorial Baptist Church in Harlem, has said, "It is my contention that prayer is 'the royal road' to church renewal."[7] Nothing much of significance in the church happens without prayer. "Unless the Lord builds the house, the builders labor in vain" (Ps. 127:1).

• *The church should demonstrate God's power.* No

one can study the New Testament without recognizing that the power of the Holy Spirit was present in the life and ministry of the first-century church. When the apostles preached, thousands came under conviction, repented, and were baptized. Even in the face of persecution and death, the church grew and thrived.

In many of our churches there is an abundance of emotionalism. In some cases it is carried to extremes. Granted, there is a place for emotionalism in church worship, if it is stimulated and controlled by the Holy Spirit and the Word of God. But emotionalism worked up through human effort is utterly devoid of spiritual profit or edification.

We face a crossroads for the black church: hope for families in crisis lies in the presence, teaching, fellowship, and ministry of the church. Yet before we can fulfill our divine role, we must experience personal and corporate renewal, opening ourselves to the power and ministry of the Holy Spirit. As Washington says, the black church "needs new zeal, new purpose, new self-image, new leadership."[8]

It is this renewal (spiritual housecleaning and reordering) that gives us the authority, power, and love to reach beyond our doors to the hurting community without. "Renewal is not just what goes on inside the four walls of the church building. As transformation becomes contagious, it tends to raise the consciousness of next-door neighbors in the community as much as it does the folk in the church. Renewal also helps a congregation overcome its sense of isolation and powerlessness as it begins to build coalitions with other churches, social service agencies, and political groups. The name of the game in renewal ministry is God's power unleashed to transform institutions as much as it changes individuals and families."[9]

## A Call for Godly Leadership

Renewal begins with our pastors and leaders. Much harm is being done to our churches because many of them have as preachers those who have entered a "profession" without first having a "possession" of God in their lives. A conspicuous failure in the ministry today, as we have mentioned, is the lack of upright, moral, righteous lives in the pulpit.

Preachers and pastors are human, just like other people. They make mistakes; they experience tragedies. But if we as pastors fail to confess our weaknesses and repent of our sins, live godly lives, we help create the criticism and indifference toward the church on the part of the people. As long as we have ministers who have shattered homes and marriages and are poor role models as husbands and fathers, the church will not reach those families who need our preaching and teaching, love and support.

Many black families, therefore, are leaving our traditional black churches. They join other black and even white churches where the Bible is preached and taught, and whose Christ-centered church programs inspire, educate, and help all ages of people. Still a growing number of others reject Christianity because of racist attitudes and actions practiced against blacks in many white churches. They join non-Christian religions and cults where they look for commitment, integrity, strength, sincerity, and discipline in what they are trying to do. These people shrug and say, "What's the church doing that makes a difference? Some preachers are the greatest con artists around." And they point to the preachers who live in palatial homes and drive expensive cars, but have little or no real compassion for the needs of the people.

If the leaders of the church do not "walk their talk," it has a devastating effect on the family. The Apostle Peter wrote to first-century pastors, "Be shepherds of God's flock that is under your care, serving as overseers—not because you must, but because you are willing, as God wants you to be; not greedy for money, but eager to serve; not lording it over those entrusted to you, but being examples to the flock" (1 Peter 5:2-4).

**163**

Pastor, are you clear about your "call" from God? Or are you in the church because some other vocation fell through? If God has called you to be a pastor, you are the shepherd. You must live a life well-pleasing to God before your people. The same is true of deacons, elders, choir members, and teachers. God has called us to lay down our lives for the flock of God, to lead them and care for them.

## A Relevant Message

Across America today there are multitudes of black church members who are hungering for sound preaching and teaching from the Word of God. They are spiritually undernourished because they're not getting "food for the soul and mind." Many of our young people are college students; they've been trained to think but when they come to some of our churches, they discover that the preachers don't have a satisfying message. Their sermons are not well-structured and very thin in biblical content. The main thrust is to the emotions of the people, which is turning away many educated blacks today. We need more biblical and expository preaching in our churches. We need pastors who know how to present the Word of God intellectually, in the power of the Holy Spirit, to meet the needs of people and their families in every area of life.

Because we have been an oppressed people, and continue to struggle with the effects of racism and discrimination, many churches have substituted other gospels: civil rights, racism, social ethics, politics. We may challenge our people to fight for their social, economic, and political rights in this world, but such a message does not touch their moral and spiritual life, nor does it prepare them for eternity. We must confront our people with the right priorities. Jesus said, "What good is it for a man to gain the whole world, yet forfeit his soul?" (Mark 8:36)

What then is our message? It must be the infallible, authoritative and liberating Gospel of Jesus Christ. With

John the Baptist we must preach, "The kingdom of God is near. Repent and believe the good news!" (Mark 1:15) Repentance for our sins for neglecting the commands of God, for failure to acknowledge Jesus Christ as our Savior and Lord—this is where our message begins.

Today there are many who will say, "That's pie-in-the-sky religion; we have to meet the needs of the people." Yes, we must, but we must decide on our starting point. God says, "If My people who are called by My name, will humble themselves and pray and seek My face and turn from their wicked ways, then will I hear from heaven and forgive their sin and will heal the land" (2 Chron. 7:14).

Our land today is sick. God wants to heal our land, including our families. But we must humble ourselves and repent of our sins that are hindering the work of His Holy Spirit. If the condition of mankind could have been changed through the self-efforts, then Christ's coming to earth was a waste of time. But no, Christ had to come, die on the cross, and through His death on the cross, burial, and resurrection, we can be reconciled with God and with each other. When men and women get right with God, it will affect their family life, their relationship to society, and all other aspects of life. This is the message that declares the truth, that demonstrates power.

We as pastors and evangelists must become true prophets of God to this generation. Then we can say as Jesus did: "The Spirit of the Lord is on me, because He has anointed me to preach good news to the poor. He has sent me to proclaim freedom for the prisoners and recovery of sight for the blind, to release the oppressed, to proclaim the year of the Lord's favor" (Luke 4:18-20).

Some people interpret this verse only in the spiritual sense; others see it as a call to social action. But it is our own spiritual heritage that shows us the intimate connection between salvation and social action. James Stalling, in his book *Telling the Story: Evangelism in Black Churches*, says, "It is upon the reception of a new life, liberated from

**165**

spiritual bondage, that Christian slaves and former slaves could then enter into a more authentic quest for political liberation."[10] He then goes on to quote from *The Conversion Experiences of Black People in Slavery and Freedom:*

> It was out of this spiritual freedom that [Harriet Tubman] decided to move toward her material, economic, and social freedom. It was after her experience of God's forgiveness that she was assured God would lead her and others in her race to freedom. It was at the moment of her spiritual liberation that she realized that social liberation from slavery was possible.[11]

In other words, says Stalling, personal and social salvation for her went hand in hand.

> Freedom from slavery and salvation from personal sin are closely related themes in the slave material. They are intimately connected. As indicated in the life of Harriet Tubman, the desire for social deliverance burned deep in her breast along with the desire for personal salvation. Personal and social salvation mutually influenced each other in the slave tradition.[12]

This intimate connection between the Gospel and its power to change lives and society is the key to an effective ministry to families—but can be easily distorted. We must always keep our focus on Jesus. We must bathe all our efforts in prayer, keeping our eyes on Him. We must preach Christ, walk in His footsteps, and give cups of cold water in *His* name and no other. For without Him, we can do nothing (see John 15:5).

## An Effective Ministry

Effective ministry that meets the needs of families in our communities must be twofold: *inreach and outreach.*

"Inreach" involves teaching and training our own members (adults and children) in God's Word and its relevance to marriage and family life—much as we have been discussing in this book. Special messages on the family, classes for couples, prayer support group for single parents, seminars on parenting—all of these should be an integrated and regular part of our teaching ministry in the church.

But how do we lift up our vision for stable family life, while at the same time encouraging and supporting those who have experienced brokenness? If we preach on the importance of the father in the home, will single parent families feel left out? If we emphasize the family, are we neglecting the role the extended family *and* the church has played in our cultural heritage? In *The Church in the Life of the Black Family,* Wallace Charles Smith speaks to this challenge:

> Given the American context, there is no question that one goal of a black family enrichment program must be to shore up the strength of the nuclear family. On the other hand, the nuclear family must also be seen as fully in community with and linked with others. . . . The variances may range from one-parent families in a nuclear arrangement to grandparents, uncles, aunts, or godparents serving as the primary parents for youngsters born outside the nuclear grouping.
>
> What must be remembered is that a black family enrichment program in black churches will certainly want to work toward stable nuclear arrangements as a goal for black people. . . . [In our western context] young blacks will be better able to advance economically and socially if the two-parent approach is adopted. Single parents in this culture have a difficult time making it economically. Beyond that fact, however, both biblically and theologically the two-parent model also lies at the heart of our Judeo-Christian faith.

From a faith standpoint, this one fact alone means that strengthening two-parent families must be the church's goal.[13]

One way to encourage the family in the context of the church is to provide a variety of programs to bring all ages into the church's sphere. Pioneer Clubs or Awana for boys and girls teach important skills and Bible memory. Programs for teens should be a high priority, where youth can gather with spiritually mature but sympathetic adults and taught how to cope with temptation, and how to protect themselves from the temptation of drugs and alcohol and immoral sexual activity. Youth for Christ, Young Life, and other organizations might bring the youth from several different congregations together. We should make it possible for boys and girls to attend good Christian summer camps.

Then there are activities which bring youth and adults together. Here are a few ideas:

- One of the most important might be a *mentoring program,* in which each teenager—especially those with only one parent in the home—is teamed up with another caring adult of the same sex as the teenager. The adult might attend sports or school activities the teen is involved in, go out for pizza and talk, and just be a caring presence in the teen's life.
- Include children in your *visitation teams* to the homebound or elderly—a dose of good medicine!
- Sponsor (or encourage your families to participate in) a *family camp* in the summer, getting away from the stresses of everyday life into a setting for good teaching, good fellowship, and wholesome activities.

Let's turn our attention to the second thrust of effective ministry, which is an "evangelistic and social outreach" to all unconverted and unchurched individuals and families in our community.

## Reaching Out to Families

The most effective outreach ministry is community-based. That is one reason the local church is a key element in helping to meet the black family crisis.

When I was pastor of Smoot Memorial C&MA Church in Cleveland, we had quite an evangelistic ministry, with our members going door to door to witness and invite families to our church. One afternoon as two of our ladies stopped at one house, they found the family in a deplorable condition. The plaster was falling off the walls, very little food was in the house, the father was sitting in a beat-up old chair watching a television that was on its last legs; hardly any light came into the room. There were ten children in the home—really hurting kids. Our women said, "We'd like to help you."

I went over to see the family and confirmed the report. I sent two of our men to the house to repair the walls; we gathered food and clothing for the kids and parents, and in about a month the whole family turned out to the church and it was a happy occasion when they came. One Sunday morning several members of the family came forward and professed faith in Christ. One of the men who went to this house was a professional painter; he hired the father and taught him how to paint. Finally the father started his own business as a means of supporting his large family. The primary role the church played was to support this family until they could support themselves.

Preston Robert Washington says, "The church might do well to recognize the fact that it deals with *real* people, in a *particular* location, with their *collective* sense of history and tradition. . . . The weak, defenseless, and oppressed individual, family, or neighborhood also is 'our kind of people.' "[14]

"The development of actual programs which will address the problems of the black family," says author Wallace Smith, "must be done in light of societal realities facing the black family. These realities are that as a suffering community blacks in America are significantly worse off than whites in the areas of health, jobs, education, and housing."[15]

Smith points to Maslow's "hierarchy of needs" as a helpful understanding of evaluating basic needs and preparing hearts for the Gospel. In Maslow's theory, certain basic needs must be met before an individual or family can begin to address needs on the next level. For instance, the most basic need level is physical: food and shelter. The Apostle James challenged, "Suppose a brother or sister is without clothes and daily food. If one of you says to him, 'Go, I wish you well; keep warm and well fed,' but does nothing about his physical needs, what good is it?" (James 2:15-16) Our faith must reach out in action.

Praise God for the black churches which are reaching out to the hurting families in their communities, growing out of their primary message of Christ's redemption, not as a substitute for it. They include:

● Rock of Our Salvation (Evangelical Free) Church (the Rev. Raleigh Washington, pastor), located in the Austin area of Chicago. The church not only shares a building with Circle Urban Ministries (Glen Kehrein, director), but the church and CUM are partners in ministry. "CUM does a lot of what the Rock isn't equipped to do but needs to be involved in—such as health care and legal aid," Kehrein says. "Likewise, CUM . . . needed a pastor and a church that could provide spiritual nurturing to people who came to CUM."

● Faithful Central Baptist Church (Dr. Kenneth Ulmer, pastor), on the border of turf claimed by two of Los Angeles' most violent gangs—the "Rolling Sixties" and the "Hoover Street Crips." The church both offers support to families that have been affected by gang violence and has formed an intervention program called Jeopardy: the police provide names of at-risk juveniles; the church members make contact with the families and follow through.

• Voice of Calvary Fellowship (John Perkins, founder) in the inner city of Jackson, Mississippi. This church believes that if Christians are going to make a witness in the black communities, they must demonstrate that the people who bear the name of Christ must be reconcilers and not dividers. This integrated church fellowship and ministry provides emergency relief to hurting families through its Agape Center. Voice of Calvary trains future leaders through its Harambee Youth Program, and addresses the critical housing needs in the area through Adopt-a-House—a program which renovates housing and sells them to families below cost, making homeowners of people who would otherwise be at the mercy of slumlords.

• The First Church of God in Christ in Evanston, Illinois (Rev. Michael Curry, pastor). This church recently dedicated their new counseling center, The Lighthouse, which provides a drug hotline, counseling for pregnant teens, and other support services. One of these is a support group for men called "Brothers in Crisis." The thrust of BIC is "Brothers in Christ" ministering to "Brothers in Crisis," coming alongside and giving support in the whole range of critical issues facing black men today—unemployment, low self-esteem, drug and alcohol abuse, broken family relationships. The goal is not only to provide resources for dealing with the crisis, but to provide spiritual hope.

In addition, there are such churches as the Bible Way Church and Third Church of God in Washington, D.C. and the Abyssinian Baptist Church in Harlem—both reaching out to their communities. But *every* black church should be such a lighthouse of spiritual hope, pointing people to Jesus Christ, the Savior. Each one of us can begin right where we are to be God's cup of cold water to hurting families. It begins with prayer, encouraged by the Holy

Spirit, prayer calling on God to renew our lives, our leaders, and our churches. And then prayer that God would give us the vision and resources to be God's family to His hurting children.

## Some things to think about and do:

1. Pastor and church leaders, have you experienced the redeeming work of Christ in your own heart and life? Are you an example to your flock of what it means to be a godly person in the church and at home?

2. Is there a small group of people who could meet regularly for prayer and Bible study to seek God for the work the Holy Spirit wants to do through your church in evangelizing your community with the Gospel of Jesus Christ?

3. What is the primary message of your church? Does your message depend on changes in society and government to help people, or is your message the Word of God, which gives hope, happiness, and deliverance even in the midst of devastating circumstances?

4. Pastor or youth worker, could you set up a mentoring program for children without fathers in your congregation? (Or Christian father, is there a youth from a single-parent family you could "adopt" as a mentor and friend?)

5. What are the most pressing needs of the families in your community: housing? absent fathers? unemployment? poverty? health? drug or alcohol abuse? wife and/or child abuse? child care? In what ways is your church helping to address these needs? Or in what way might your church begin to address these needs?

6. Will you believe God's promise for these needs—"Call unto Me, and I will answer thee, and show thee great and mighty things which thou knowest not" (Jer. 33:3).

# - 12 -
# The Survival of the Black Family

*Done made my vow to the Lord*
*And I never will turn back.*
*I will go, I shall go,*
*To see what the end will be.*
        *Traditional*

**The assault on the family** from every side is real. The very survival of the black family is at stake. During the Third National Summit on Black Church Development, Mike Faulkner said, "The crisis [in black America] is of such magnitude, it behooves us as African-American churchmen to call upon God on behalf of our nations for healing."[1]

And yet we have hope. As long as the Gospel is being preached, as long as there are churches reaching out to their communities with a relevant ministry, there will be Christian families who are building their foundations on the Solid Rock. We take exception to the critics who are saying that the family is doomed. Yes, the family is in crisis; it is being buffeted in the storm, but it will not be destroyed! The family will survive the struggle.

Having said that, however, we must ask how the black family can keep its identity and be restored when it's threatened on every side? How can the ship stay afloat?

## Keep the Old Landmarks

When a ship is battered at sea, it finds its way by familiar landmarks that can be trusted. The same is true of the family. Although we must adapt to our ever-changing culture, it is vitally important that we are not simply adrift, or we will end up broken on the shoals of selfishness, sinfulness, and perversion. We must keep on course, our goal set by the Word of God, keeping the old landmarks in sight.

"Remove not the ancient landmark, which thy fathers have set," warned the writer of Proverbs (22:28, KJV). But we must be deliberate about keeping the biblical landmarks, because they are being systematically dismantled. Some people are declaring that the family based on Judeo-Christian principles is on its way out. Sexuality is simply a matter of "preference"; live-in partners should have the same legal rights as spouses; homosexual "families" are "just another alternative." "Husband" and "wife" have been replaced by the term "sexual partner" in sex education literature; the schools, social agencies, and government are seen as the responsible parties in caring for our children instead of the home.

There are other landmarks which have served us well, which have guided us through many difficult periods. The autobiography of John H. Johnson, owner of Johnson Publications, which publishes *Jet* and *Ebony,* refers frequently to many of the ancient landmarks which have guided many of us through difficult times and situations. Says one author who reviewed his book, "Johnson grew up in poverty in Arkansas and spent some time on welfare in Chicago, but he believed that if he was willing to work hard on a single goal that he could make something of his life. Show me a black family which has moved from poverty to prosperity, and I will show you people who have followed *the ancient landmark of hard work* [emphasis added]."

Johnson's story is also one of overcoming many personal and societal obstacles. Says the author, "Somebody must hold up this ancient landmark: life is not easy. . . . When the obstacles come along and we are set back, how do we respond? Do we give up and settle for something less? . . . Or do we remember the ancient landmark that the race is not to the swift, or the battle to the strong, but to him who endureth to the end?"[2]

A choice stands before us. We can throw up our hands and let the tides of popular culture and the storms of social foment throw us about where they will. Or we can keep the ancient landmarks clearly in our vision, and let them move us forward into our inheritance as black families. Remember Moses' challenge to the people as they stood at the crossroads between the wilderness and the Promised Land:

> See, I set before you today life and prosperity, [or] death and destruction. For I command you today to love the Lord your God, to walk in His ways, and to keep His commands, decrees and laws; then you will live and increase, and the Lord your God will bless you in the land you are entering to possess.
>
> But if your heart turns away and you are not obedient, and if you are drawn away to bow down to other gods and worship them, I declare to you this day that you will certainly be destroyed. . . .
>
> I have set before you life and death, blessings and curses. *Now choose life, so that you and your children may live* (Deut. 30:15-19, emphasis added).

Benjamin L. Hooks, executive director of the NAACP, puts some of these ancient landmarks in perspective: "Adherence to traditional civil rights action remains as vital as ever, but for many in our society, something extra is needed. No need seems more urgent than the recapture and restoration of old and cherished values—decency, morality, hard work and education—by which the majority of black Americans once directed their lives."³

Knowing our heritage, owning our pilgrimage, even through the dark days of slavery, reclaiming the spiritual strength that has enabled us to endure, opening up God's Word in our hearts and our homes—all are part of keeping the landmarks clearly fixed.

It's true that the crisis in the black family looms so large that many problems seem beyond our control. It's easy to feel *hopeless* because we feel *helpless* to do anything about our problems. But instead of resigning ourselves to victim status, many black leaders are saying it's time for African Americans to take action.

### We Must Take Control of Our Own Destiny

William Raspberry, columnist for *The Washington Post,* wrote: "A myth has crippled black America; the myth that racism is the dominant influence in our lives. Two things flow from this racism-is-all myth. It puts the solution to our difficulties outside our control. And it encourages the fallacy that attacking racism as the source of our problems is the same as attacking our problems."⁴

Raspberry doesn't deny that racism and all its attendant evils have thrown roadblocks into the path toward success for African Americans. But he challenges the attitude that we must wait for white America to get its moral act together before we can do anything about the crisis in our communities and families. "Let's say you're exactly right," he tells black leaders, "that racism is the overriding reason for our situation and that an all-out attack on racism is our most pressing priority. Now let us suppose that we eventually win the fight. . . . What would you urge we do next? . . . Well, why don't we pretend the racist dragon has been slain already—and take that next step right now."[5]

Joe Clark, who gained national attention for his tough discipline while principal of Eastside High School in Paterson, New Jersey, says, "I have noted that a growing number of concerned blacks refuse to accept the cries of historical deprivation; they blame 'Whitey' and 'the system' as the root causes for the decline in the basic fabric of black life. These people want to be *consequential* to society as opposed to being a *liability* to society. In essence, Marcus Garvey probably put it most profoundly, 'Up, up, you mighty race, you can accomplish what you will!'[6]

Clark directs his challenge especially to black men. "It is time for blacks to take charge of their fate. . . . Being a highly optimistic individual, I state emphatically that the situation can be repaired with assiduity and conviction. This cannot take place until acknowledgement of this plight is accepted. Probably the root cause is the breakdown of the family structure. . . . Without strong black men at the helm of the ship, its ultimate rendezvous will be with doom."[7]

The Rev. Fred Shuttlesworth, cofounder of the Southern Christian Leadership Conference (SCLC) and pastor of Greater New Life Baptist Church in Cincinnati, told a group of African-American leaders at the Ohio Black Expo in August 1990: "We have gotten so lazy that we let government agencies raise our children. Those responsibilities belong to black families and black churches. The leaders in our communities must take control again."[8]

At the same gathering, capital city SCLC president, Jerome Jordan, said that the black church must work in conjunction with community organizations to improve the conditions of black Americans. Jordan said SCLC's goals are to make sure the black church is no longer a "sleeping giant" in the community. Shuttlesworth agreed that "taking control" must include a spiritual renewal: "A few people whose hearts are determined can turn a world upside down, but God must be at the center of our struggle."[9]

The voices of African-American women are being raised in mutual accord. "We should neither ask nor accept that other races of people hold themselves responsible for what happens to our youths," says Janet Ballard, a leader in the national organization Alpha Kappa Alpha. "No, our actions must demonstrate that blacks will take the leadership—with all of the help and resources available—to save our children."[10]

As African-American leaders in our communities—parents, pastors, youth directors, and laypeople—we must unite in a strong message to our young people: *Take advantage of existing opportunities.*

Columnist William Raspberry says: "It is beyond arguing that black Americans, especially youngsters in the inner cities, have fewer options than justice requires. But it is also true that too many of them fail to avail themselves of the opportunities that do exist. . . . I don't mean to suggest that desperately poor youngsters . . . should be blamed for all their bad choices. But the society that shares the responsibility is much closer at hand [than white society]: parents, teachers, ministers, journalists. All have to help drive home to these young people the simple fact that even their limited options hold the potential for turning their lives around."[11]

The Rev. Tryone Crider, speaker at Central (Ohio) State's Convocation in 1989, urged students, "Stop talking about your dreams and goals and start doing whatever you want to become." He also strongly urged them to take control of their own lives. "Young ladies, say, 'No, I didn't come here to get a baby; I came here to get a degree.' . . . What is more important, rapping or reading, discoing or discovering? You've got to make good choices . . . you've got to be strong." Crider continued as he encouraged the students to avoid self-destruction, to not give up when times get tough, to always do their best, be mentally alert, and let God be their best friend. "He is a good friend to have. You ought to take God with you everywhere you go.

You cannot make it without God on your side."[12]

These and other respected black Americans today are sounding a common theme: hope is renewed when we take responsibility for our own attitudes, actions, and choices. "When people believe that their problems can be solved, they tend to get busy and solve them."[13]

## We Must Strengthen the Cords

All of us feel inadequate in the face of the forces battering the black family today. But that's not such a negative state. When the Apostle Paul was struggling with weakness, God told him, "My grace is sufficient for you, for My power is made perfect in weakness" (2 Cor. 12:9). When we admit our weaknesses, we open ourselves to the power of God working through us to strengthen the cords that bind our hearts and homes.

It's important to ask God to show us how to get our homes in order by strengthening the priorities and relationships in our own homes and families. One way to do this is with a family checkup. You might use this book as the basis for such a checkup, discussing the questions at the end of each chapter with your spouse, family members, or a support group of parents at church. Sometimes pastors, counselors, or marriage enrichment programs have a "marriage checkup" that couples can do together.

The point is to set aside time, get away from other responsibilities, and talk and pray together about your spiritual foundation, family priorities, communication, unity on discipline of children, family activities. Are there conflicts that need to be resolved? Are there relationships that need to be reconciled?

Above all, we want to encourage you, husband and wife, mom and dad, single parent or grandparent, to strengthen the cords by reading the Bible and praying together. It is through prayer that we share our hearts with God.

Networking is important. There is a story about an ancient warlord who wished to pass on his kingdom to his twelve sons. But his sons were a quarrelsome lot, each trying to outdo the other, and quick to take advantage of his brother's weaknesses. The dying warlord called his sons together, gave each an arrow, and asked if they could break their arrows. Puffed with pride, each young warrior easily snapped his arrows. Then the old man bound twelve arrows together and asked each son to try to break them. One after the other grunted and strained, but not one could break the bundle of arrows. They thought they had failed. But the father said, "If you keep on quarreling among yourselves, each one looking out only for himself, you will be broken as easily as you broke the single arrows. But if you lay aside your quarrels and work together, no one will be able to break apart this kingdom from your rule."

Our individual efforts may seem like a drop in the bucket in helping turn around the fathers of our black families. But if we discover one another, share our resources, and work together, we can strengthen our cords and become a powerful force for change. In business terms, this is called networking.

Janet Ballard, quoted earlier, says, "Blacks can save our youths by reclaiming the institutions through which we can function totally on our own . . . , by becoming the models they so desperately need. We must return to networking with traditionally black churches and organizations. Black Americans must, in coalition with each other, identify the causes that are destroying our youths. We must eliminate these causes from our own adult lives and become the models our youths can emulate."[14]

The Detroit-based Institute for Black Family Development under the leadership of its president, Matthew Parker, is committed to equipping existing church leaders to strengthen families within their own congregations. To meet this objective, the institute produces materials and conducts seminars to help empower pastors and laymen and women with resources which they can take back to their own congregations. (See "Resources for the Black Family" in the back of this book.)

The Institute also believes that part of the crisis facing the black family is that the underclass, in particular, has lost the vision for what is possible. If all you see around you is failure, you will simply learn failure. To learn success, you need models of success. Some of the solutions to the crisis in the black family are being generated by the black community itself, including black churches. Part of the Institute's task is to identify individuals and Christian organizations in the black community dealing with the problems of the black family in imaginative and innovative ways—and bringing churches and concerned black leaders together to share ideas and resources and develop shared objectives and mutual cooperation.

In reporting on the Third National Summit on Black Church Development, mentioned earlier, *Christianity Today* said: "One major result of these informal meetings has been to enable black-led urban, rural, and overseas evangelism ministries to discover one another."[15]

A similar consortium of some 200 black ministers from Michigan to California gathered in Los Angeles in July 1989 for the Harambee Pastors Summit *(Harambee* is a Swahili word meaning "let's pull together"). "And pulling together is what black America has to do," said ministers gathered for the summit, if problems such as drug abuse, teen pregnancy, and unemployment are ever going to be properly addressed and controlled within inner-city communities. "We don't want to be spiritually on welfare or physically on welfare," said Harambee president Chuck Singleton, a Fontana, California minister, who added that the church could succeed where governmental programs have failed. "We believe solutions to problems in black America lie in black America."[16] The Rev. Kenneth Ulmer, chairman of Harambee and pastor of Faithful Central Baptist Church in Los Angeles, said, "Prior to the 1950s there was a spiritual focus on solving these problems only. In the '60s and '70s there was a social focus only. But now, we realize it's not either/or, but both/and."[17]

In order to strengthen the cords for an increasingly demoralized black underclass, each of us must find ways to reach out and give a hand to our brothers and sisters who are floundering in the inner cities. John Johnson, the publisher of *Ebony* and *Jet* mentioned earlier, in commenting on the responsibility of the black middle class, said, "I think all of us have to reach back—for very selfish reasons. I don't think black people, be they rich or poor, will ever be free until we are all free. I have done very well for myself, but not a day goes by when I am not reminded that I am black. [Singer] Paul Robeson once said he could never go anywhere as Robeson that he couldn't go as a black man. We have to fight for the respect of all blacks, before we can get it ourselves."[18]

There's a great need for black American lawyers, doctors, musicians, artists, athletes, business people, and others to return to the inner city and put something back into the community. A recent television program featured a prominent black lawyer in Washington, D.C., a former "ghetto kid," who went on to school and bettered his education. One day he visited one of the blighted areas where he was born and felt a real commitment to do something for the kids. He went back and gained their confidence, formed a baseball team, bought them uniforms, etc. One day one of the kids said to him, "We appreciate what you're doing for us. We know you don't live here anymore. Some of us were wondering what you're in to." The kid smiled slyly. "You must be one of them cocaine kings."

The lawyer was shocked. "Why would you say that?"

They shrugged. "You drive a fine car, you come and go as you please. We decided you must be dealing drugs."

Only then did it dawn on the lawyer that these kids had only limited role models; either you were down and out, or you were "making it" dealing drugs.

Moses McClendon, national president of Phi Beta Sigma, says, "Each of us, and particularly black men, must move immediately to re-involve ourselves in some type of religious community. We must seek out the remnants of the previously existing youth training organizations and become volunteers. We must recognize that the inner-city urban areas have become desolate because of our departure and the withdrawal of our talents; and we must re-establish our connection with these communities. *We must become personally involved.*"[19]

And Regina Frazier, national president of The Links, Inc., argues, "Positive role models are still our most effective weapons in an arsenal that seeks to convince youths that they must set long-term goals, and then have the tenacity to bring those goals to fruition. Life is a cyclical experience. As such . . . each of us reaching down and pulling up . . . will erode the societal stratification of class delineation."[20]

Another cord that must be strengthened is the education of our young people. Douglas Wilder, governor of Virginia, and also cochairman of the Commission on African-American Males, discussed this matter in an interview with *USA Today's* Barbara Reynolds. Note some of his insightful comments:

> Our societal values across the board have just disintegrated. Take the movie *Wall Street,* where the leading character says that greed is good. It is money, bucks. No one is saying the good life comes as a result of years of planning, saving for a college education for your kids, a sacrifice for your generation so the next generation will be better. All that's gone. So this affects all Americans, but disproportionately African-Americans because they have less family immunity to that kind of harm.
>
> Education is key. We've got to make certain that

opportunities exist for college and to improve what we do in vocational education.

[We must] provide opportunities and help them assume responsibilities. But give them values. Those values have to come from a family setting. Where there's no home, we've got to provide the surrogate support system, and that could only come from the community, from the neighborhood.

Our parents always told us: You can be whatever it is you want to be as long as you don't waste your opportunities, as long as you become as educated as you can become. Don't waste your time. Do your homework and respect the rights of others. Respect family because it's the one thing that will stand with you in the years to come. And understand that man is not the keeper or the maker of his destiny. There is a superior being.[21]

Dr. Rejesta Perry (Sigma Gamma Rho) helps focus where the responsibility for education lies: "Enforcing quality education in schools is the job of parents, black organizations and churches, which should act as self-appointed watchdog groups . . . making sure that black children, wherever they are educated, receive an appropriate distribution of funds for their education."[22]

How can parents encourage quality education? At home. "Students must learn to balance social activities and academic activities. One way parents can increase their children's academic activities is to help them develop good study habits. Once your child develops and internalizes good study habits, they will be rewarded with better academic achievement. . . . The rewards for academic achievement will lead to a successful career."[23]

Yes, we must be involved in the schools. Yes, we must vote appropriate legislation to improve the quality of education our children receive. Yes, we must support community action to keep gangs and drugs out of our schools.

But in the meantime we can help our children take the attitude of the principal who told students who complained about this or that teacher, "There never was a teacher who kept me from getting an education."

Parents, set aside study time; enforce it. Turn off the TV and music during this time. Read with your children; play learning games; look at maps of different parts of the world and helpful features that are in the news. Insist on regular attendance at school; be in contact with your child's teachers. Quality education begins in our homes.

Probably nothing makes parents feel more helpless than the drug menace that is unraveling our children's future faster than we can strengthen the cords of protection around them. But there is a critical role that parents must play. As Jesse Jackson said in an interview with *Ebony* magazine, "The government can cut the *supply* of drugs, but 'we the people' must cut the *demand* for drugs."[24]

Drug abuse is connected to many of the other problems plaguing our homes and communities. Many crimes—assault, robbery, burglary—are committed by people who need money to support their chemical addiction. The lure of big bucks selling drugs short-circuits educational and career goals. Drug trafficking is often behind gang-related violence. And, says Jackson, "Drugs, not sexual contact, have become the chief transmitter of AIDS. Drugs and crime are directly related. Drugs are dream busters and hope destroyers."[25]

Part of the problem, Jackson says, is that we aren't mad enough yet. "I visit high schools and talk with students, and I often ask them what they would do if someone brought little ropes and KKK sheets and spread them out on the table at their next party. They unanimously say they would immediately run that person away from the party. Then I ask these same students, 'What would you do if someone brought some drugs—a little cocaine, a little "snow"—to the party and spread them out on the table?' They usually say something like, 'Well, I'd tell them to go in the other room; don't do that stuff around me.' In other words, the response is less clear and less than total rejection. Our minds and our morals do not reject dope to the degree that we reject the rope. Yet we are losing more of our young people to dope than we ever lost to the rope!... Dope pushers live in our neighborhoods and try to pass themselves off as our friends. Our total community must reject the dope pushers and see them as terrorists. We must change our minds, our morals, and our conduct."[26]

Actor Tim Reid, vice chairman of the Entertainment Industry's Council for a Drug-Free Society, has said, "No one is forcing anyone to snort anything through their nose, or inject anything into their veins or swallow anything to get high. That's coming from people's own needs and weakness. The crime syndicate is just taking advantage of that weakness. What has to change is black people's attitude toward drugs.... We can't use racism as a catch-all for all the ills of our community. Drugs are illegal. Anybody who deals in drugs should pay the price, be they white, black, or any other color."[27]

Without holding white racism blameless, Dr. Lorraine Hale, director of Hale House, a haven for drug-addicted children, says that in the final analysis, "It is up to black people to rid themselves of this antisocial menace."[28]

What can parents do? Search Institute reports that there are "six factors which research and experience suggest are important components in preventing adolescent chemical abuse."[29] They are as follows:

*1. Parent expectations.* Alcohol and drug use is relatively low among adolescents whose parents set strict rules about chemical use, monitor compliance, and enforce the rule.

Mom or Dad, do you insist that *all* parties and teen gatherings be drug and alcohol free? Do you require reasonable curfews? Know the warning signs of possible drug or alcohol use? What are your kids learning by your own example?

*2. Peer influence.* Chemical use or nonuse is strongly related to what one's friends do. Parents can undermine the negative influence of friends both by steering children away from certain associations and toward other relationships where the influence is known to be more positive.

Parents, get to know your child's friends! Invite them to your house (yes, yes, it's noisy and they eat a lot—but it's important to know who your child's friends are). Offer to drive them places. Throw parties at *your* house where you can supervise.

*3. School environment.* Chemical use tends to be lower among adolescents in schools where there are firm policies about drug use and where these policies are maintained and enforced.

Parents, do you know what your children's schools are doing to educate students and combat drug abuse among the student body? Find out; insist on education for both students and parents. Band together with other parents to demand removal of gang (and drug-related) paraphernalia at school. Insist on "closed campuses" or whatever it takes to keep drug pushers out.

*4. Social networks.* The degree to which adolescents are involved in adult-supervised programs and activities is another factor which inhibits chemical use.

Encourage your child to get involved in youth activities at church, or positive activity groups at school, the local park district, and community center. If at all possible, provide music, art, sports activities, or other special interests. It's less expensive in the long run than hanging out on the street corner.

*5. Social competency.* A number of social skills, all of which can be promoted by family, school, church, or other organizations, can serve as important factors in prevention. These include friendship-making skills, communication skills, decision-making skills, and the ability to say "no" when peer pressure mounts.

Parents, keeping your kids under lock-and-key is not the answer to surviving adolescence. Young people need to experience making decisions—even if sometimes they make the wrong choices. But if you give them increasing opportunity in areas that are not moral issues or life-threatening (what to wear, choice of activities, how to spend their own money, etc.), they will be better able to make good decisions in areas that count.

*6. Personal values.* Adolescents who refrain from alcohol and drug use, in comparison to other youth, are more committed to education and educational achievement, more involved in people-helping activities, more confident that the future holds promise, more affirming of religion, and more able to resist immediate gratification of needs.

In short, the very things we have been encouraging in this book. Reclaiming our spiritual heritage, acknowledging our need for God, getting our priorities straight, building up our own marriages and homes will go a long way toward strengthening the cords of protection around our young people, enabling them to resist the insidious pressures of the drug culture.

Does this happen overnight? Of course not. Each individual family and our communities as a whole have a long uphill fight. It's easy to get discouraged. But we don't have to wait until all the problems are solved.

### We Can Renew the Hope

For the Christian family, we find hope in God's promises to stand by those who put Him first in their lives and obey

His commandments, even when it means bucking society's values. The Apostle Paul encouraged the early Christians, "Marriage should be honored by all, and the marriage bed kept pure, for God will judge the adulterer and all the sexually immoral. Keep your lives free from the love of money and be content with what you have, because God has said, *'Never will I leave you; never will I forsake you.'* So we say with confidence, *'The Lord is my helper; I will not be afraid. What can man do to me?'* " (Heb. 1:4-6), emphasis added).

Paul mentions several big problems which are destroying the family—sexual immorality, love of money, and discontentment—and says that none other than the sovereign God, Lord of lords, King of kings will be our helper! We don't have to fear! Our God is bigger than the crisis!

Fear and faith are very similar in that they both stem from a belief in what's *going* to happen. Fear, however, destroys while faith builds up.

This doesn't mean that just because we as a family have faith, we will not have problems or suffer in the crisis. David, whom God had promised would be king of Israel, spent years running for his life! But he never gave up hope; he clung to the promises of God; he remained faithful to God and God remained faithful to him. "Be strong and take heart," David wrote, "all you who hope in the Lord" (Ps. 31:24).

At one point in his life David blew it; he committed adultery, then covered it up with murder. But when confronted with his sin, he repented and God restored His blessing. You may feel you've blown it too. But it's never too late to turn back to God and turn your family around.

Hope is the turning point. Do we believe the crisis in the black family will consume us? Or do we believe that your family and our family, your church and our church, with the power of God, can make a difference? It is up to us to restore hope, not only to this generation, but to the ones to come. The psalmist wrote:

[The Lord] commanded our forefathers to teach their children, so the next generation would know [His commandments], even the children yet to be born, and they in turn would tell their children. Then they would put their trust in God and would not forget His deeds but would keep His commands. They would not be like their forefathers—a stubborn and rebellious generation, whose hearts were not loyal to God, whose spirits were not faithful to Him (Ps. 78:5-8).

With God's help, we *can* break into the vicious cycles which are sucking our families into crisis. We can overcome someday—and that someday is now. It is up to us. "I have set before you life and death, blessings and curses. *Now choose life, so that you and your children may live and that you may love the Lord your God, listen to Him, and hold fast to Him*" (Deut. 30:20).

Will you join us in choosing life?

**Some things to think about and do:**
1. Do you believe the answers to the crisis facing the black family can be found in the black community? Why or why not?
2. In what ways do you feel like a victim of societal attitudes and government regulations? In what ways might you change from victim-status to taking control of your own destiny?
3. Brainstorm ways you might join forces (networking) with other churches and organizations to strengthen black families. Contact one or more of the organizations in the Resources section of this book for ideas.
4. What gifts and resources do you have that you might be able to "give back" to inner-city youth, communities, schools, churches? Make a plan to invest yourself back into the black community in some way in the next year.
5. Parents, what can you do to encourage good study habits and educational activities in your own home?

**6.** Of the six factors mentioned which inhibit drug abuse among adolescents, which ones need special attention in your home?

# Endnotes

**INTRODUCTION**
1. William Raspberry, "The Myth That Is Crippling Black America, *Reader's Digest,* August 1990, p. 97.
2. Excerpted from testimony of Don Lewis, director, The Nehemiah Family Project, before the Select Committee on Children, Youth, and Families, U.S. House of Representatives, July 25, 1989.

**CHAPTER 1**
1. *They Stopped in Oberlin,* by William E. Bigglestone (Scottdale, Pa: Innovation Group, Inc., 1981).
3. Wanda Jones with Sandra P. Aldrich, *Living in Two Worlds — The Wanda Jones Story* (Grand Rapids: Zondervan Books, 1988), p. 16.

**CHAPTER 2**
1. Albert J. McQueen, "Adaptations of Urban Black Families," *The American Family,* edited by David Reiss, M.D. and Howard A. Hoffman, M.D. (Plenum Publishing Corp., 1979).
2. Robert B. Hill, *Strengths of Black Families* (New York: Emerson Hall Publishers, 1972).
3. Andrew W. Edwards, "The Black Family: A Unique Social System in Transition," *The State of Black Cleveland, 1989* (Cleveland, Ohio: Urban League of Greater Cleveland, 1989), p. 187.
4. Andrew Billingsley, *Climbing Jacob's Ladder* (New York: Simon & Schuster — Touchstone Books, 1990).
5. William Raspberry, *The Washington Post* (n.d, n.p.)

## CHAPTER 3

**1.** Edwards, "The Black Family" (see chap. 2, n. 3), p. 192.

**2.** Statistics from "Understanding African-American Family Diversity," *The State of Black America 1990,* published by National Urban League, 1990, pp. 97–99.

**3.** "Restoring the Black Family," *Family Policy,* a publication of the Family Research Council, September/October 1989.

**4.** *Ebony,* Special issue: "The Crisis of the Black Family," August 1986, p. 37.

**5.** Andrew Billingsley, *The State of Black America 1990,* National Urban League, 1990, pp. 97–98.

**6.** See note 4 above, p. 53.

**7.** Niara Sudarkasa, "Black Enrollment in Higher Education: the Unfulfilled Promise of Equality," *The State of Black America 1988* (Cleveland, National Urban League, Inc., 1988), p. 10.

**8.** Wade Nobles and Lawford Goddard, "Drugs in the African-American Community: A Clear and Present Danger," *The State of Black America 1989* (Cleveland, National Urban League, 1989), pp. 163–64.

**9.** See note 4 above, p. 149.

**10.** Ibid.

**11.** "Drugs, Gangs Mix in Sinister Combination," *The Journal* (Lorain, Ohio), May 21, 1990, pp. 1, 5.

**12.** Ibid.

**13.** "A Dialogue with Eleanor Holmes Norton," *Emerge,* August 1990, p. 12.

**14.** Marilyn Miller Roane, "Drug Money Drives Gangs," *The Beacon Journal* (Akron, Ohio), October 17, 1989.

**15.** Ibid.

**16.** Ibid.

**17.** Regina Brent, "Bad parenting and children," *The Beacon Journal* (Akron, Ohio), July 15, 1991.

**18.** Ben Carson, M.D. with Cecil Murphey, *Gifted Hands, the Ben Carson Story* (Zondervan, 1990).

**19.** "Who Will Do Science?" *Call and Post,* Cleveland, October 19, 1989, p. B-1.

**20.** Ibid.

**21.** "School Power: A Model for Improving Black Student Achievement," *The State of Black America 1990* (New York: National Urban League, 1990), p. 225.

**22.** Marvin McMickel, "Black Men: Endangered Species," *ClubDate,* August/September 1989, p. 29.

**23.** Kevin Johnson, "A Bold Experiment for Educating Black Males," *USA Today,* October 11, 1990, p. 4-D.

**24.** Ibid.

**CHAPTER 4**
**1.** Billingsley, *The State of Black America* (see chap. 3, n. 5), p. 90.
**2.** See chap. 3, n. 2, pp. 89–90.
**3.** Edwards, "The Black Family" see chap. 2, n.3) p. 186.
**4.** Ibid., p. 188
**5.** See chap. 3, n. 4, p. 50.
**6.** *Family Policy,* September/October 1989, a publication of the Family Research Council, quoting *The Non-Suicidal Society* by Andrew Oldenquist (Bloomington: Indiana University Press, 1986).
**7.** "Those of Broader Vision: An African-American Perspective on Teenage Pregnancy and Parenting," by Georgia L. McMurray. *The State of Black America 1990* (Cleveland: National Urban League, 1990) pp. 195, 202, 204.
**8.** Joan Wester Anderson, "Sex Respect—A New Program for Teens," *Liguorian,* May 1989.
**9.** See chap. 3, n. 4, p. 62.
**10.** Sources: Bureau of the Census; National Center for Health Statistics; Bureau of Justice Statistics; the Sentencing Project as quoted by *Newsweek,* October 15, 1990, p. 67.
**11.** "Celeste Appoints Forty to Study Plight of Black Males," *The Call and Post* (Cleveland, Ohio), May 25, 1989, p. 8-C.
**12.** Ibid.
**13.** Ibid.
**14.** See chap. 3, n. 22.
**15.** Susan B. Griffith, "Commission to Study Problems of the Black Male," *The Call and Post* (Cleveland, Ohio) September 14, 1989, p. 2-A.
**16.** Alvin F. Poussaint, M.D., "Save the Fathers," *Ebony,* August 1986, p. 46.
**17.** Ronald E. Childs, "The Strong Black Man," *Ebony Man,* February 1990, p. 61.
**18.** Mark V. Reynolds, "A Search for the Endangered Black Man," *New Visions,* October/November 1989, p. 14.
**19.** "The American Black Family: A Christian Legacy" (video), Summit Productions, Detroit, Michigan.
**20.** Ron Williams, "Consider This," *The Call and Post* (Cleveland, Ohio), October 5, 1989, p. 3-C.
**21.** "Project 2000" on CBS' "60 Minutes," October 7, 1990.
**22.** Denworth and Wingert, "Can the Boys Be Saved?" *Newsweek,* October 15, 1990, p. 67.

**23.** William Raspberry, "Bring Back the Family," *The Washington Post,* July 18, 1989.

**24.** George Gilder, "Welfare's New Consensus: The Collapse of the American Family," *The Public Interest,* Fall 1987, p. 21.

**25.** John W. Miller, *Biblical Faith and Fathering: Why We Call God "Father"* (Mahwah, New Jersey: Paulist Press, 1989), pp. 13–17.

**26.** See note 23 above.

**CHAPTER 5**

**1.** Adapted from *Living in Two Worlds—the Wanda Jones Story,* (see chap. 1, n. 2).

**2.** Paul Ciotti, "Why Are Men Going for the 'Lite' Relationship?" *The Los Angeles Times,* as reprinted in *The Journal* (Cleveland, Ohio), June 28, 1987, p. 34.

**3.** See Leviticus 18:22; 20:13; 1 Corinthians 6:9-20; Romans 1:21-27.

**4.** Jerry B. Jenkins, *Hedges—Loving Your Marriage Enough to Protect It* (Brentwood, Tenn.: Wolgemuth & Hyatt, 1989).

**CHAPTER 6**

**1.** Sermon by Tony Evans, Oak Cliff Bible Fellowship Church, Dallas, Texas. Replayed on "Focus on the Family" radio broadcast, September 21, 1990.

**2.** Sermon by Tony Evans on the "Focus on the Family" radio broadcast, March 22, 1989.

**3.** Lee Quency Broadous Green, from the foreword to "The Thirteenth Triennial Family Reunion" of the late Reverend & Mrs. Z. Broadous, Sr.

**CHAPTER 7**

**1.** "A Time to Seek," *Newsweek,* Dec. 17, 1990, pp. 50–56.

**2.** Josh McDowell, *How to Help Your Child Say "No" to Sexual Pressure* (Waco, Texas: Word, 1987), pp. 99–100.

**3.** "A Promise with a Ring to It," *Focus on the Family* magazine, April 1990. The Durfields founded For Wedlock Only. See the Resources section in this book.

**CHAPTER 8**

**1.** Jawanza Kunjufu, "Children Are the Reward of the Life" (Chicago: African American Images, 1982).

**2.** Armand M. Nicholi, Jr., "What Do We Know about Successful Families?" a pamphlet published by Harvard Medical School, Massachusettes General Hospital [n. d.].

**3.** Ibid.
**4.** Laura B. Randolph, "Like Father, Like Daughter," *Ebony,* June, 1989, p. 154.
**5.** "Nurturing Fulfills Fathers," interview with Dr. Kyle Pruett, *The Plain Dealer,* Cleveland, Ohio, Nov. 16, 1989, p. 15-E.
**6.** Ibid.
**7.** Nocholi, (see n. 2 above)
**8.** Sonya Henderson, "3 Strikes *for* You," *Essence,* March 1989, p. 136.
**9.** Ibid., p. 45.

**CHAPTER 9**
**1.** Gordon MacDonald, "Why Self-Esteem Is So Important," in *Parents and Teenagers,* edited by Jay Kesler (Wheaton, Illinois: Victor Books, 1984), pp. 277–78.
**2.** Adapted from *Just Me and the Kids,* by Patricia Brandt with Dave Jackson (Elgin, Illinois: David C. Cook Publishing Co., 1985), Chap. 11.
**3.** Josh McDowell, (see n. 1 above), p. 213.
**4.** Ibid., p. 214.
**5.** Adapted from "Let's Talk about Spanking," by Neta Jackson, *Family Life Today,* September 1981.

**CHAPTER 10**
**1.** Jack Harris, *The Communicator News,* Columbus, Ohio, July 19, 1991.
**2.** "The Black American Family" (see chap. 4, n. 19)
**3.** Adapted from "Overcoming Five Underlying Reasons for Divorce," by Luis Palau, *Husbands & Wives* (Wheaton, Illinois: Victor Books, 1988), pp. 465–67.
**4.** Randy and Therese Cirner, *Husbands & Wives* (see n. 3 above), p. 312.
**5.** Adapted from *The Pillars of Marriage,* by Norm Wright (Ventura, California: Regal Books, 1979), pp. 147–48.
**6.** Cirner, *Husbands & Wives* (see n. 3 above), p. 313.
**7.** Evelyn Christenson, (see n. 3 above), p. 331.
**8.** Lewis Smedes, *Forgive and Forget* (San Francisco: Harper & Row, 1984).

**CHAPTER 11**
**1.** Adapted from "The American Black Family" (see chap. 4, n. 19)
**2.** Ibid.
**3.** Wallace Charles Smith, *The Church in the Life of the Black*

*Family,* Judson Family Life Series (Valley Forge, Pa.: Judson Press, 1988), p. 22.

**4.** William E.B. DuBois, *The Souls of Black Folk* (Chicago: A.C. McClurg & Co., 1903).

**5.** Otis Moss, "The Relationship Between the Black Church and the Community in Cleveland," *The State of Black Cleveland 1989* (Cleveland, Ohio: Orange Blossom Press, 1989), p. 9.

**6.** Preston Robert Washington, *God's Transforming Spirit: Black Church Renewal* (Valley Forge, Pa.: Judson Press, 1988), pp. 19, 21.

**7.** Ibid., p. 15.

**8.** Ibid., p. 14.

**9.** Ibid., p. 16.

**10.** James O. Stalling, *Telling the Story: Evangelism in Black Churches* (Valley Forge, Pa.: Judson Press, 1988), p. 59.

**11.** Edward F. and Anne Streaty Wimberly, *Liberation and Human Wholeness: The Conversion Experiences of Black People in Slavery and Freedom* (Nashville, Tenn.: Abingdon Press, 1986), pp. 28–31.

**12.** Ibid., p. 30.

**13.** Smith, *The Church in the Life of the Black Family* (see n. 3 above), pp. 40–41.

**14.** Washington, *Black Church Renewal,* (see n. 6 above), p. 23.

**15.** Smith, *The Church in the Life of the Black Family* (see n. 3 above), p. 78.

**CHAPTER 12**

**1.** " 'Dues-paying Time' for Black Christians," *Christianity Today,* August 20, 1990, p. 51.

**2.** See chap. 3, n. 22, pp. 30–31.

**3.** "What Must Be Done," *Ebony,* August 1988, p. 162.

**4.** William Raspberry, "The Myth that Is Crippling Black America," *Reader's Digest,* August 1990, pp. 96–98.

**5.** Ibid.

**6.** Joe Clark, "It Is Time for Blacks to Take Charge of Their Fate . . . , " *Ebony,* August 1988, p. 122.

**7.** Ibid.

**8.** *The Communicator,* Aug. 24 through Aug. 30, 1990, pp. 26–27.

**9.** Ibid.

**10.** "What Must Be Done," *Ebony,* August 1988, p. 158.

**11.** William Raspberry, "Children Need to Learn Options in Life," *The Journal* (Ohio), October 30, 1987, p. 5.

**12.** *The Call and Post,* October 5, 1989.

**13.** William Raspberry, *Reader's Digest,* August 1990, p. 98.

**14.** *Ebony,* August, 1988, p. 158.

**15.** *Christianity Today,* August 20, 1990, p. 51.

**16.** Charisse Jones, "Pulling Together," *Los Angeles Times,* July 8, 1989, p. 1.

**17.** Ibid., p. 10.

**18.** Courtland Milloy, "Can the Black Middle Class Increase Aid?" *The Beacon Journal,* March 5, 1989, p. D3.

**19.** *Ebony,* August 1988, p. 164.

**20.** Ibid., p. 160.

**21.** Gov. Wilder's quote, *USA Today,* April 11, 1991.

**22.** "What Must Be Done," *Ebony,* August 1988.

**23.** W. Monty Whitney, Ph.D., *Call and Post* columnist (Cleveland, Ohio), Sept. 13, 1990.

**24.** "Down with Dope! Up with Hope!" *Ebony,* August 1988, p. 136.

**25.** Ibid.

**26.** Ibid., pp. 132–134.

**27.** "Massive Abuse of Illegal Drugs Must Be Stopped," *Ebony,* August 1986, p. 150.

**28.** Ibid.

**29.** Search Institute *Source,* Volume II, Number I, January 1986.

# Suggested Books for Further Reading and Study

*A Man's Touch,* Charles Stanley, Victor Books.

*Before the Mayflower: A History of Black America,* Lerone Bannet, Jr., Johnson, Chicago.

*Christians in a Sex-Crazed Culture,* Bill Hybels, Victor Books.

*Growing Wise in Family Life,* Charles R. Swindoll, Multnomah.

*Guiding Your Family in a Misguided World,* Anthony T. Evans, Focus on the Family.

*How to Equip the African-American Family: Issues and Guidelines for Building Strong Families,* George and Yvonne Abatso, Urban Ministries, Chicago.

*Heaven Help the Home,* Howard G. Hendricks, Victor Books.

*How to Raise Them Chaste,* Richard Durfield, Bethany House.

*How to Raise Christian Kids in a Non-Christian World,* compiled by Youth for Christ staff, Victor Books.

*How to Really Love Your Child,* Ross Campbell, Victor Books.

*The Black Family, Past, Present and Future,* Lee N. June and Matthew Parker, Zondervan.

*Quiet Times for Couples—A Daily Devotional,* H. Norman Wright, Harvest House.

*Substance Abuse,* Marion Duckworth, William Davis, and Patricia Myers, Cook.

*Straight Talk,* James Dobson, Word.

# Resources for the Black Family

This is a partial list of organizations that specialize in various helps for black families.

**Christian Family Outreach, Inc.**, Andre Thornton, president; 3101 Euclid Ave., Suite 704, Cleveland, OH 44103 (216-432-0333). Helps meet spiritual and social needs of inner-city families through summer camps.

**For Wedlock Only,** Dr. Richard Durfield, president; 1407 Foothill Blvd., Suite 307, La Verne, CA 91750 (714-592-5262). Inspired by Dr. James Dobson and his book *Dare to Discipline,* this organization provides parents with resources to have a "key talk" with their children about sexual purity.

**Institute for Black Family Development,** Matthew Parker, president; 16776 Southfield Rd., Detroit, MI 48235 (313-893-4434). Provides many helpful resources for the family.

**Joy of Jesus,** Rev. Eddie K. Edwards, executive director; 12255 Camden, Detroit, MI 48213 (313-839-4747). Reaches out to youngsters through camping, counseling, and a special school.

**Camden House,** Mary Edwards, program director; 12017 Camden St., Detroit, MI 48213 (313-526-9290). Features a comprehensive program emphasizing all phases of daily living.

**Lighthouse,** Michael Curry, director; 1607 Simpson St., Evanston, IL 60201. Operates a substance abuse hot line (708-328-

0973) or 328-0764), plus support groups that meet at various times.

**Nehemiah Family Project,** Don Lewis, director; 5 Thomas St., N.W., Washington, D.C. 20005 (202-667-6728). Works with dysfunctional families through counseling and with black men to help them be responsible husbands, fathers, and community leaders.

**Urban Alternatives,** Dr. Anthony Evans, president; P.O. Box 4000, Dallas, TX 75208 (800-800-3222). Supplies resource material to help families live God's way.

**"Why Wait,"** Josh McDowell Ministry, P.O. Box 1000, Dallas, TX 75221 (214-234-0645). Features extensive resources—tapes, books, high school programs, etc.—to help teenagers learn how to say no to sexual pressure.

**Home Ministries,** Ron Ballard, director; 2752 Churchland, Dayton, OH 45406 (513-274-2670). Ministers to families through various means.